How to Write Amazing Essays

The Complete Guide to Essay Research, Planning, Writing, Structuring and Formatting

Dr Josh Martin

Academy Works
www.academyworks.co

Published by Academy Works,
an imprint of Penlyn House.
www.penlyn.co

Copyright © 2023 Josh Martin
All rights reserved.
ISBN: 9781739401610

Table of Contents

1. Writing Amazing Essays 3
- 1. The Bedrock of Academia 3
- 2. The Essay Production Process 5
- 3. Truly Benefiting from Feedback 11

2. The Brief 15
- 1. Following Assessment Instructions 15
- 2. Understanding Assessment Criteria 26
- 3. Types of Essay 36

3. Your Argument 39
- 1. Critical Thinking 39
- 2. Making a Persuasive Argument 50
- 3. Forming an Argument 55
- 4. Developing Your Own Essay Topic 60

4. Research 65
- 1. Embracing the Researcher Lifestyle 65
- 2. The Source Hierarchy 71
- 3. Expert Tips on Becoming an Efficient Researcher 80

5. Planning 95
- 1. Always Be Planning 95
- 2. Argument Sequencing 100
- 3. Producing Your Essay Outline 104
- 4. Get Ready to Write 109

6. Structure 111

   1. The Fish Skeleton 111
   2. Signposting and Signalling 114
   3. Paragraph Structuring 117
   4. Sentence Structuring 126

7. Introduction and Conclusion 131
   1. How to Write an Introduction 131
   2. How to Write a Conclusion 138

8. Writing Properly 145
   1. The Building Blocks of an Essay 145
   2. Becoming an Excellent Writer 146
   2. Common Writing Problems 152

9. Writing Approaches 175
   1. Writing in the First and Third Person 175
   2. Concise Writing 180
   3. Reflective Writing 196

10. Referencing 203
   1. The Importance of Referencing 203
   2. Footnotes and In-Text Citations 204
   3. Referencing Styles 213

11. Formatting 221
   1. The Principles of Good Formatting 221
   2. Formatting Rules to Follow 224

12. Further Resources 235

About the Author 243

1. Writing Amazing Essays

1. The Bedrock of Academia

Much of what you know about writing essays is probably wrong. I can say this because I have taught thousands of students, at many universities and at all levels, and most did not understand how to write essays effectively. Every year, thousands of students discover that writing essays is not as simple as they once thought, and that it's nothing like how they learned it in school. In fact, writing amazing essays is like learning a new language: there are hundreds of very specific rules and conventions that students are expected to learn and follow. Unfortunately, these rules are rarely understood, let alone known about.

It is hard to overstate the importance of essays within academia. For millennia, they have represented the most significant and effective medium for expressing academic arguments, ideas and findings. They are the lifeblood of academia and even your professors will usually publish their research in the form of an essay. They are also the principal form of assessment for students, especially at university and beyond. The ability to write powerful essays is *fundamental* to academic practice and no student can achieve excellence without achieving complete mastery of the essay.

As a result, students spend a huge portion of their time at university trying to improve their essay writing skills, in the knowledge that this has a huge impact on their grades. We have all been in a cohort that has those lucky students who seemingly do less work than everyone else, but who still outperform others. Many students wonder what their secret is. I can tell you: it's not what they know, it's how they organize and communicate what they know. You can work hard to learn everything there is to know in your subject, but if you do not know the essential secrets, tips and hints of essay writing, you are unlikely to get a good grade. It's that simple.

It's no wonder it gets confusing for students. Many of the things we expect you to do in academic essays are rarely set out for you. Searching online is hopeless, given that there is too much conflicting information that is usually inaccurate or poorly explained. In fact, much of what you see online has been written just to hit certain "keywords", to help improve the Google rankings of different ecommerce businesses. It's often not written by an expert on the subject (more often it's students!). Meanwhile, your academic tutors rarely have the time to sit down and explain everything to you. It's no wonder that students struggle.

Fortunately, if you are a student in any discipline and at any level (from undergraduate to postdoc), then this book finally shares with you all the secrets and tips on delivering amazing academic writing. I can guarantee that following its advice will improve the quality of your academic work and will drive up your academic grades, as well as make your study more enjoyable, efficient and satisfying. It covers every aspect of the essay production process, from understanding your assessment brief, to formulating your arguments, conducting research, developing critical analysis, planning, structuring, writing, referencing, formatting, and much more. At every step along the way I have included super helpful to-do lists, summaries, tables, examples and diagrams. These are based on years of experience teaching students how to perfect essays and so have been subject to much refinement. Instead of only *talking about* what you need to know, this book lists *hundreds of effective tips* to give you clear action points to follow.

These tips will not only improve the quality of your work, but could significantly improve your essay writing efficiency, your overall mood and the quality of your academic work life. With the small investment of the day or so needed to read it, this book will give you a complete and truthful picture of the academic essay "language". After reading it, like learning a language, you will continuously improve by practising all the points in the book and can use it as an ongoing reference guide throughout your studies.

I am a university lecturer who has successfully coached thousands of students across all levels—from those beginning at university right up to postdoctoral students—on how to transform their academic work. I have worked at three leading universities in the UK, while also being an in-demand private tutor across the world. I have designed and delivered many successful academic modules, as well as graded thousands of papers. I pride myself on my ability to break down complex ideas and to give students simple steps they can take to achieve their aims. I have always been especially dedicated to improving my students' essay writing. Now it's time to share that knowledge with the world.

2. The Essay Production Process

This book takes you right the way through the essay building process, from the initial stages when you first receive your brief, right up to the moment you press *Send*. The essay production process is richer and more complex than many people realize, with multiple stages and steps that need to be considered along the way. I like to break the entire process down into nine steps beginning with the letter *F*. These steps can be further conveniently grouped into three stages: the Research Stage, the Writing Stage, and the Final Stage. I shall explain each of the steps, as well as how they are covered in this book.

The Research Stage: Foundations, Framing and Focusing
(1) Foundations
When students first receive their assignment brief there is sometimes a sense of panic and often the question, "Where do I even begin?" It's important to realize that this initial uncertainty and unfamiliarity is entirely normal and human. In this first stage, I always advise my students to start with the very basics. You

should try to enjoy the process of being a newbie to the essay's subject matter and with becoming familiar with its foundational elements. Great places to start are your course materials, tutorial notes or lecture recordings. Similarly, go to the easiest textbooks on the subject, looking at chapters or sections dedicated to the subtopic in question, as well as read things like Wikipedia. At this stage it's not even about "research", but about familiarizing yourself with the subject matter, the relevant issues and debates, and any terminology. Getting this foundational understanding of the subject allows you to build on top with deeper, analytical research.

(2) Framing
This is the next stage in your research journey, where you begin going deeper on specific ideas and starting to compile research notes on relevant ideas, arguments and research findings. It is about starting to get a sense of the field of enquiry, as well as the shape and contours of the debates within. At this stage, you will move on from the foundational materials and will advance to critical secondary sources and literature in the field, including peer-reviewed journal articles, edited volumes, reports, monographs and other key sources. You will also start to get a sense of what your argument is and the direction of your paper.

(3) Focusing
This is where you start to formulate your own views, critical perspectives and arguments from the literature. You synthesize what you are reading and start to map out your essay skeleton and core arguments. Now you have a clearer view on our core arguments and the direction and aims of your thesis, you can also be more focused on sourcing all the materials needed. This means more specifically targeting materials and literature that backs up or supports your critical analysis. For essays that involve some empirical or practical component, it's also the stage at which you conduct any primary research and begin drawing together your analysis and findings.

1. Writing Amazing Essays

I have broken this first Research Stage down into these three steps to emphasize that quality research does not start happening right away. It takes time and persistence. The more you read, plan and immerse yourself in your subtopic, the more focused and effective the research will be. It's all about continuously building up in layers, starting at the very basics.

Chapters 2 to 5 are dedicated to supporting students across the research phase of their essays. Chapter 2 looks in detail at understanding assignment briefs, as well as understanding the key skills and elements that are being assessed in your essays. Chapter 3 goes into detail on the importance of critical analysis and the formulation of a persuasive and robust argument. Chapter 4 is dedicated to research skills and how to become an effective and efficient academic researcher, as well as exploring practical skills like time management, self-discipline and organization. Chapter 5 is dedicated to essay planning and drawing out a skeleton of your essay, so that you are ready to get writing.

The Writing Stage: Forming, Finding and Fixing
(4) Forming
This is essentially the write up stage. Now that you have an essay outline and have compiled all your key findings, materials and sources, it's time to start writing. As explained later, this stage is so much less daunting once you have completed the earlier Research Stage. When you have produced a detailed skeleton for your essay, where you know what each section is going to argue, as well as the sources and materials you will be using, the writing stage is actually quite enjoyable! It's important to also note that, while I have it here as a single "step", writing is really an ongoing process. You are likely to come back to this stage a few times and you should certainly expect to tweak your plan as you move forward, as well as refine one or two early drafts of your essay. It sounds like a lot, but it is this focus and rigour which is what produces outstanding essays. Furthermore, the more you do it, the quicker and more natural it becomes.

(5) Finding

This is a simple step to remind you that, while writing, you may not necessarily have *everything* you need. You may occasionally spot gaps in your literature or materials, which require you to dip back into the library and databases to source further points. Or, quite simply, you might have left some gaps in your essay for links, materials and resources which you know can be accessed easily when it comes to it. This might include references for your sources, for example. While writing we may occasionally need to fill these gaps.

(6) Fixing

The final step in the Writing Stage is the equally important fixing of your essay. This is largely combined with formatting (coming next), but is focused more on improving the substance, quality and delivery of your essay. Excellent essays are never the product of the first or even second draft: they are usually made from ongoing and continuous tweaks and perfections to the layout, construction and execution. This requires plenty of proofreading, editing and polishing, as well as spotting errors or areas where the delivery is not as effective and needs refining.

The Writing Stage of Forming, Finding and Fixing is covered comprehensively throughout this book. Chapters 5, 6 and 7 are dedicated to matters of essay structure, paragraph structure, argument sequencing, transitional language and the effective development of your narrative. Chapters 8 and 9 cover great detail on effective academic writing skills, including grammar, punctuation, writing tenses, concise writing and reflective writing.

The Final Stage: Formatting, Final Submission and Feedback

(7) Formatting

Now that we have our almost complete manuscript, that is been worked through and refined, we need to run final checks and complete document-wide formatting. This means making sure that the essay is professionally presented and has consistent and accurate formatting throughout. It also means general tidying, gap-filling and final checks for writing precision and delivery. We can also, at this stage, complete our detailed references in the bibliography or footnotes.

(8) Final Submission
This step is included to illustrate the point at which you have finally completed everything, put your essay into the correct format and have finally pressed *Send*.

(9) Feedback
In fact, the process is not over when you press *Send*. After receiving your grades back, it's crucially important that you dedicate time and focus on digesting and understanding the feedback you receive. Perfecting your academic work is not done overnight but takes lots of practice, as well as through multiple opportunities for feedback and improvement. The feedback you receive on your academic papers is gold dust when it comes to the value it can bring to improving your essay writing. Feedback therefore feeds into your future essays and thereby creates a cycle between all these F's, as follows:

How to Write Amazing Essays

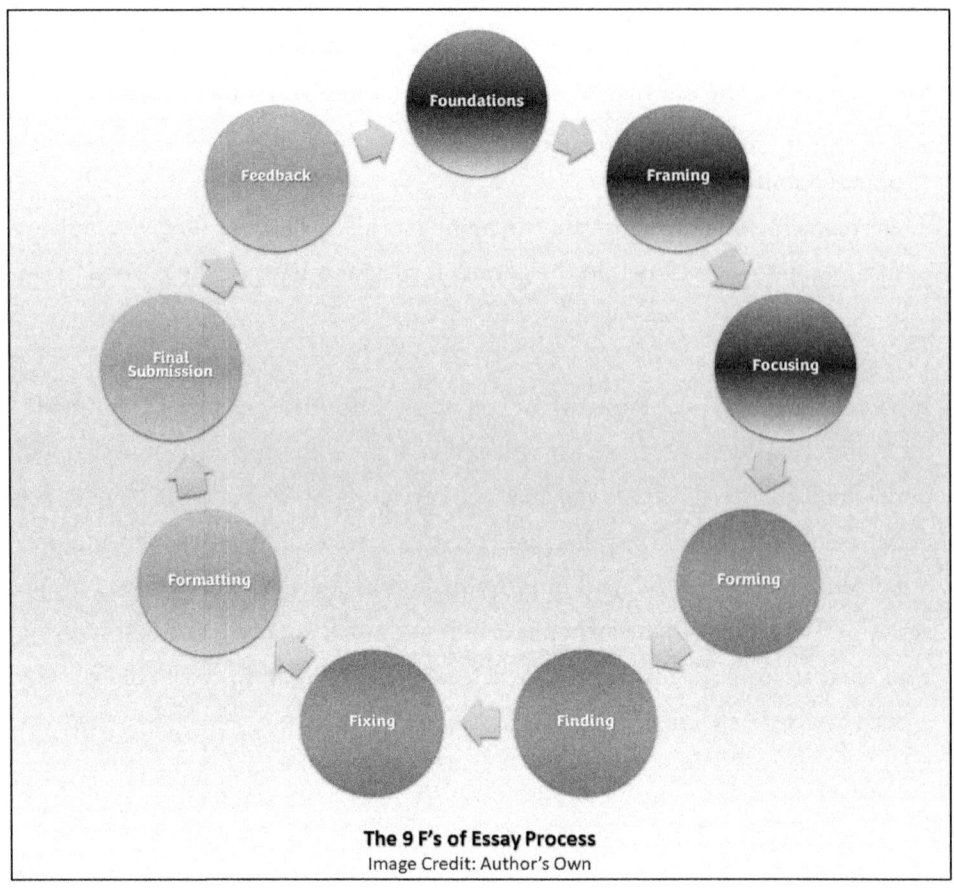

The 9 F's of Essay Process
Image Credit: Author's Own

The final three steps of Formatting, Final Submission and Feedback, together comprising the Final Stage, are covered throughout the book. Chapter 10 is dedicated to referencing and gives students a deeper and precise understanding of how referencing works in academia, as well as dozens of tips on mastering referencing styles, conventions and practices. Chapter 11 is dedicated to essay formatting: a subject that is all too often neglected in academic guides, but which is essential to producing a quality, persuasive and effective paper. Finally, given that Feedback is the step that arises before the beginning in this process, it seems fitting to cover advice on it here in Chapter 1.

3. Truly Benefiting from Feedback

Reading everything in this book will help transform your essay writing skills. However, nobody becomes an excellent essay writer overnight. There is no magic pill and the main ingredients you need are perseverance and practice. Academic success is built upon repeated opportunities to check your learning and by powerful action planning in response to *feedback*. Feedback helps you shape, perfect and steer your academic progression. The better you manage and process feedback, the more quickly and effectively you master academic study. It is therefore essential. Fortunately, the following tips will help you get the most out of your feedback.

✓ **Take all opportunities for feedback**

Feedback can come in many forms and at many stages. You can receive informal feedback by attending and engaging in seminars and lectures. You can engage with formative (unassessed) assessments and activities. If you meet with your tutor, you can get feedback in that way. Feedback also includes self-reflective work (see Chapter 9) and your own research into methods of improvement, including reading this book. Equally, by submitting your assessments, you can usually acquire formal feedback on your essays. Keep in mind all these different forms and types of feedback, from formal to informal, and maximize your opportunities to acquire it whenever you can.

✓ **Cross-check feedback against your assessment**

When reviewing your feedback after an assessment, check your submission to look at the specific elements to which the feedback refers. It's very easy to skim over feedback and not absorb it effectively if you do not examine how or where it applies. Going back inside your essay will reinforce your learning and will ensure that you have a precise and accurate understanding of the feedback. You can also cross-check the feedback against the assessment criteria and your institution's marking guidelines (see Chapter 2), helping you identify which criteria have been met and the specific areas that need work.

✓ Develop an action plan for your next assignment

It is important to understand that "feedback" is in some ways an oxymoron: the main purpose of feedback, really, is to feed forward! It is focused on helping you do even better in your future work. Make sure, therefore, to actually take your feedback forward. Pause a moment and spell out the exact changes or fixes you need to make in future assessments. It might even help to draw out an action plan or bulleted list of things that need work. Have a clear plan in mind and consider how you will address issues with specific steps or strategies. Make sure to revisit the action plan again when you are working on your next assignment.

✓ Try to take feedback constructively

It is easy to be disappointed, frustrated or even upset by some feedback. We have all experienced it when hard work leads to gloomy or discouraging feedback. Try not to let your emotions take over or make you despondent. Remember that academia is all about scrutiny: your tutors work in a world of giving and taking constructive—even challenging—feedback. Recognize that their feedback is *only* intended to *help you* improve. What is more, tutors all have a different style and a different tone in their writing: some are just more direct and abrupt than others. Avoid adding emotions into the language. Instead, focus as much as possible on the content. This helps you remain positive and focused, as well as ensure that your response is more rational and practical.

✓ Take note of positive feedback

It is natural to take more notice of negative feedback, than positive. Negative feedback is more jarring, and we feel it more deeply. As mentioned, try to remove those emotions and see it as a fantastic opportunity to achieve excellence. Also, make sure to really take stock of the *positive* feedback you receive. It is important

1. Writing Amazing Essays

to give yourself a huge pat on the back at the work you are putting in, as well as to remember your individual strengths and areas of progress. What is more, the areas you excel in can provide that vital foundation upon which you can build your broader success. Indeed, every academic has their own style, approach, voice and technique. Identifying your strengths helps you understand what kind of academic you are.

✓ **Consult the marker for more specific feedback**

If anything is not clear, you should consult the marker (if you can) to improve your understanding about what specifically needs improving and suggestions on good practices to adopt. Do not feel bad about using your tutor's time in this way. I often remind students, "That is what I am paid for!" Your tutor should be able to give you tips, clues and ideas on ways to improve. Do not expect them to immediately remember the specific paper or the feedback they gave you, as they probably mark lots of papers. I therefore recommend emailing them a copy of your assessment and feedback before the meeting or taking in a copy with you. They may also need a few minutes in the meeting to go back through it. If possible, think of specific questions or areas you want guidance on beforehand.

✓ **Maximize feedback by coming back to relevant parts of this book**

After reading this book, your grades should significantly improve. However, I also recommend referring back to relevant parts of this book again to help address anything specific in the feedback you receive. For example, if your feedback says that you need to improve your argument or critical engagement, then refer again to Chapter 3. If it points to your research quality and use of materials, refer again to Chapter 4. If it discusses issues around structure, clarity and narrative, then re-read Chapters 5 to 7. If it discusses problems of communication, writing or presentation, then go back to Chapters 8, 9 and 11. If it points to referencing, then refer back to Chapter 10. In all cases, go back again to Chapter 2, which provides detailed insights on the different marking criteria and expectations we have, as markers and scrutineers, of your essays. You may also find the academic assessment glossary (which you can download for free at **academyworks.co**) super helpful, as it explains a lot of different assessment and feedback terminology.

2. The Brief

1. Following Assessment Instructions

Before anything, it is crucial that you accurately follow your assignment brief. Not only is 'answering the question' a vital assessment criterion (see below), but failure to address the precise topic your tutor is pointing to, or to demonstrate a specifically required skill, is likely to undo your hard work in all other areas.

Spend Time Re-Reading Your Instructions

You must spend a lot of time making sure you fully comprehend the precise instructions and expectations for your essay assignment. Far too often, students read the assessment instructions once or twice and then steam ahead without looking back. You should be making constant reference back to the assessment instructions, to double-check that you have stayed on track. For example, I would suggest you need to: read the assessment instructions when they arrive, as well as review any additional guidance or support; after processing them, review them a second time while working in the 'Foundations' stage of the cycle (see Chapter One); develop a plan for your essay, referring back occasionally to the assessment instructions to check you are on track (in the 'Framing' stage); start structuring out your essay, checking that your proposed structure and flow of argument conforms to the instructions (in the 'Focusing' stage); then, half way through writing, perhaps even check the instructions again (in the 'Forming' stage); and, once you come to sign off your conclusion and finalize your paper in the 'Fixing' stage, you may need to read them again!

I know this sounds excessive, but it's so easy (and so human) to create false memories and false connections between words and instructions, which can lead to later misinterpretations. Therefore, keep going back to the source to check you have not gone off the tracks. Without doing this, all the hard work could be lost through a simple and easily remedied error.

Begin Reviewing Your Assessment Instructions as Early as Possible

There is also the question of *when* you should start planning or preparing for your assessments. The answer is, without any doubt at all, from the *immediate moment* they are released. This does not necessarily mean that you need to start writing or making notes for the assessment immediately, but that you should start the process of understanding the assessment and what it will require, while also thinking about ways to tackle it. There are three extremely good reasons for this.

- ❖ First, remember that you ultimately have two parts of your brain constantly working: the conscious and subconscious mind. Our subconsciousness does a huge amount for us every day, both good and bad. While you may only be able to appreciate your conscious thoughts, your subconscious brain is also rapidly firing away all the time, even while you sleep. This is why we often think of good ideas or solve problems over the fullness of time; or why they just appear to us while we are doing something completely different, like eating a sandwich. It's also exactly why people often say to 'sleep on it' when trying to solve a problem or arrive at a decision. I would rely on my subconsciousness a huge amount when doing an assessment and, with an added benefit, I was not even aware of the work being done by my brain *in the background*. Get to grips with your assessment early and begin thinking of ideas and brainstorming with your conscious mind. Occasionally go back to it consciously, to keep moving ideas around. All the while, during this time, your subconscious mind will be beavering away, working on ideas for you too!

- ❖ Second, remember that a hugely critical aspect of academia is building your skills of time management, self-organization and planning. By having a very clear understanding of what is required in upcoming assessments, as well as the work that you need to put in to achieve your desired grade, you will have the most accurate information on the timescales involved. This can be kept under review, as you continually plan out your schedule for the coming weeks. Refer back to my 9 F's of Essay Process in Chapter 1, to get an idea of the different stages that need to be incorporated into your planning. Knowing what is likely to be coming up at each stage enables you to get a clearer idea of the timescales involved.

- Third, it might be stating the obvious, but the sooner you start work on your assessment, the more time you have. Giving yourself more time allows you to maximize every stage of the essay process, as well as to break it up into neater components that fit better around your schedule. You will also have more time to clarify your understanding, perhaps even discussing the assessment with peers or checking instructions with your tutor. If you email your tutor 48 hours before an assessment deadline with a question, it will probably be too late, and the answer will certainly arrive too late for you to take corrective action. More time also means greater opportunity to locate suitable resources, such as arranging inter-library loans or ordering books. Get ahead of the game early.

Read This Whole Book

The best advice I can offer to understanding what is being asked of you is to read this whole book. Given that it offers a huge amount of detail on what is specifically expected from students, as well as clear explanations and instructions on how to tackle common assessment challenges, it could be one of the most valuable things you could read throughout your studies. What is more, it will give you a lot of insight and understanding about what the expectations might be in any essay assignment brief.

Understand Key Words and Directions in Your Instructions

To help deconstruct and clarify your essay question, you want to look out for the different key words and directions within the wording. In particular, it is often said that an essay question is comprised of **process** words, **content** words, **evaluative** words and **limiting** words.

Process Words (or Directive Words)	Provide a specific process or method for you to adopt. They are usually words that instruct you to *do* something. For example, are you being asked to "compare and contrast", "argue", "discuss", "identify", and so on.
Content Words (or Substance, Subject or Topic Words)	Identify the key subject area(s) of focus in your essay. It is these areas that form the broad topic of the essay and the areas where you need to demonstrate critical knowledge, understanding and awareness of the literature. Usually these are topics or sub-topics from your module learning.
Evaluative Words	Ask you to *evaluate*, *quantify* or *qualify* a particular proposition, argument or approach. Is something "accurate", "effective", "fast", "slow", "efficient", "strong", "weak" and so on. Alternatively, is something the "most" or "least", such as "fastest", "slowest", "most effective", "most impactful", "most ground-breaking", and so on.
Limiting Words (or Focus or Scoping Words)	Limiting words are much like an addition to the content words, but they operate by limiting or defining the scope of the content. For example, they tell you to focus on a particular region, timeline or subtopic, such that they "limit" the scope of the subject. They may also include additional areas of focus, such as specific materials or databases that must be consulted.

2. The Brief

You will notice that process words are usually *verbs* (e.g., argue, discuss, analyze, evaluate, and so on), evaluative words are usually *adjectives* (e.g., fast, effective, weak, informative, and so on), and content words and limiting words are usually *nouns*. Understanding the distinction between all these terms will really help you to deconstruct and fully understand what is being asked of you. For example:

- Process words will help you to determine what kinds of critical thinking and analysis you need, as well as the types of data and evidence you will need to successfully carry out the process.
- Content and limiting words will help you determine the relevant literature, debates and knowledge you need to focus on within your research, as well as helping shape the boundaries of the subject matter.
- Evaluative words will help you to determine whether you are producing an effective, persuasive and relevant argument in response to the question.

The different words will collectively help you determine a relevant argument (see Chapter 3), as well as ensure that you are advancing that argument or position in your essay. In terms of evaluative words, it's also worth approaching them with a sense of nuance. Think of them to the extreme: if a question asks if something is the "most effective", then you are not exploring whether it is just effective, but whether it is *most* effective. If the question asks if something is accurate, then you should be questioning if you can punch any holes in that idea at all.

Process Words

The content, evaluative and limiting words are often easier for students to interpret than process words. A student will likely be familiar with the subject matter of the essay, as it will often form part of their course learning. If they are not familiar with the specific subject matter, a quick bit of Googling and reading across your textbooks should clarify the topic area. Similarly, students usually understand evaluative words, which are often standard adjectives used in day-to-day language. Process words, however, are more complex. For these, it is worth having a more detailed explanation for the common words and phrases, as provided in the Assessment Terms Glossary (downloadable at academyworks.co). In the majority of cases, as you will see, the focus is firmly on generating an *argument* in response to the question set. For example, even if a question says to "compare", "comment" or just "discuss" something, it often really means, "form an *argument* in response to". Make sure you always cross-check your process words against the assignment brief glossary, to ensure that you are developing your arguments effectively against the precise instructions.

Essay Question Examples

To help illustrate these points, let's look at some examples.

"The Covid-19 pandemic has had a positive impact on social mobility in the workplace. Critically discuss."				
Process Words	Critically discuss	**Content Words**	Covid-19 Pandemic / Social Mobility
Evaluative Words	Positive impact	**Limiting Words**	In the workplace

It is quite common to have a statement which is followed by a process word, like here. We are therefore being asked to "critically discuss" or, in effect, develop a perspective and write a persuasive thesis on it in relation to this question. It should therefore be clear from your analysis what the argument or conclusion of your paper is. The evaluative words—"positive impact"—are asking us to be critical and to ask ourselves critical questions on this point: Has it made a mixture of positive and negative impacts? Could its positive impact be seen in a different light? Is its "positive impact" absolute and unqualified? The content words are reasonably obvious, being Covid-19 and social mobility, as well as focusing specifically on issues "in the workplace". However, it's vitally important that a student structures their discussions around the *argument*, not the topic. Be careful not to write an *exploratory* essay that just discusses interesting critical points on social mobility in the workplace following Covid. It must only use this as the subject and context for the *argument*. See more in Chapter 3.

"Compare a formal versus substantive conception of the rule of law. Which is a more accurate portrayal of the rule of law and why?"			
Process Words	Compare / Which is	**Content Words**	Formal vs substantive views of rule of law
Evaluative Words	More accurate portrayal	**Limiting Words**	None

The content and topic of this essay is also clear. It appears unrestricted by any limiting words and, given the nature of this topic, a student may even be permitted to look at different geographical regions and time periods. There are two processes involved here: "compare", followed by "which is more accurate". In both cases, we are looking for a *critical* account of *both* conceptions that looks, particularly, at developing a picture of which is more accurate. It is not about having the *correct answer*, but about producing an argument on one side or the other that is persuasive and effective. If you are asked a question like "which is more", then make sure it is crystal clear from your discussions which side your essay is taking. As explored in Chapter 3, it is okay to have arguments or conclusions that are qualified. For example, you might argue that a formal conception is *generally* more accurate, *except with regard to…* and so on. It's perfectly okay to not be 100% of one view, just make sure you clearly identify a *view*.

"Critically assess whether artificial intelligence will revolutionize education in the future."			
Process Words	Critically assess	Content Words	Artificial intelligence / Education
Evaluative Words	Revolutionize	Limiting Words	In the future

Another pretty standard essay question. "Assess" is a common process word that invites the student to critically examine a topic or question, with a view to formulating a persuasive argument on the matter. Here the subject is clearly artificial intelligence (AI) and education, with a particular focus on *future* education. Given that we need to produce an argument on this topic, it would be important to not venture off into discussing AI more broadly for the whole essay. Apart from supplying necessary meaning and context, most of the substance and analysis should be focused *specifically* on AI in the classroom, with a particular view to future likely impacts. Remember, evaluative words, like "revolutionize" here, need to be reviewed hypercritically. It's not asking whether AI will *impact* or *improve* future education; it's asking whether it will *completely transform* it into a new paradigm entirely.

"Trace the socioeconomic factors that played a role in the outcome of the UK's European Union referendum (Brexit) result. Evaluate whether social pressures or economic pressures played the most significant role."			
Process Words	Trace / Evaluate	Content Words	Socioeconomic factors / Brexit referendum
Evaluative Words	Played a role / Most significant role	Limiting Words	UK / Social and economic pressures

This essay looks complex, but it can be seen in a much simpler light: it is ultimately asking the student to critically examine the causes of the Brexit vote outcome, as well as determine whether social or economic pressure was the greater force between the two. The process word "trace" is usually asking you to critically examine the *causes* or *sequence of events* that led to the outcome (see Academic Assessment Glossary at academyworks.co). The argument formulated by the student needs to assess or "evaluate" the most significant factors and it needs to have a clear view which is stronger between social or economic pressures. As above, it does not have to be 100% in favour of one view and could deliver an argument that sees different elements of both: it just needs to make that argument and intended conclusion clear throughout.

Some Final Tips on Interpreting Your Essay Question

Remember, the most important aspect of understanding assessment instructions is to make sure you read them fully, along with all the supporting guidance, multiple times and as early as possible. Some further steps and suggestions for enhancing your understanding of the assessment are as follows:

✓ **Listen to everything about the assessment intently**

Keep a keen ear out in lectures and in class for any signposting or hints regarding the assessment. If a class includes any discussion on the assessment or its subject matter, you should try to attend and fully engage. Similarly, you should read all the surrounding instructions and guidance for that assessment.

✓ **Crossmatch your instructions with your module learning**

Assessments are rarely looking to trip you up or send you down an unfamiliar path. While it's not always the case, you will most often find that the assessment is based heavily on discussions or prior work that has taken place on the module. When reading your assessment, think of any obvious links between the assessment topic and an issue or debate previously covered on the module. Nine times out of ten, the assessment will have been covered in some kind of critical discussion or debate on the course, so this is fertile territory for inspiration and somewhere you should venture back to, to build up your notes, research sources, ideas and understanding.

✓ **Try to be aware of who is marking your assessment or who set the assessment**

While we follow strict processes to ensure marking consistency, there are always small elements of subjectivity that can creep in. For example, anyone who knows that I will be marking their paper would be well-served to ensure that the piece is well-presented and does not contain sloppy writing. Whereas some tutors can be more lenient on this, I am firmer. Therefore, take close note of any dominant interests of your tutor or any idiosyncrasies that they might have. Again, using me as an example, you can get a firm word from me if you are using footnote referencing and insert the footnote number before the full stop, like this[1]. By contrast, I knew one colleague who would mark harshly if a student did not put their bibliography into the correct format, which is something I am less likely to lose sleep over. (And yes, I probably have lost sleep over the footnotes.)

✓ **Think also about the marker's or assessment writer's interests**

Is there a particular source, author, rule, theory, argument or debate they keep coming back to or seem to spend a long time discussing? You can be sure these might be things the tutor is interested in and expecting you to take an interest in too. On this point, many students have asked me if they should align the political or ethical angle of their essays to conform to the politics or ethics of the marker. For example, imagine a situation where your tutor is a vocal right-wing libertarian, but your essay is making arguments in favour of socialist ideas. This can be an understandably tricky situation for a student. The first thing to say is that your tutor *should be* objective. As an academic, it is their job to leave their personal politics at the door and to always mark from a neutral position.

2. The Brief

It really comes down to the power of your argument. I have given excellent grades to papers promoting political ideas in contrast to my own, because they were well executed papers that were persuasively written and clearly backed up with reference to evidence. But I agree this is somewhere you need to tread carefully. If you are directly flying against a marker's stated beliefs, you would do well to make extra sure that you show a deep and nuanced understanding of the counterview (i.e., their view!) and can effectively challenge it with persuasive evidence. For example, use studies or academic articles that offer a rebuttal that you can shield yourself behind. Of course, you must never make arguments that are clearly harmful or toxic, such as promoting racist, sexist or violent thinking, even if you think you can find a compelling basis. I know this sounds extreme, but having worked with colleagues on thousands of papers, I have seen it all.

✓ **Be wary of over-relying on your peers' notes, ideas or essay plans**
I am a firm believer in student cohorts working together as much as feasible throughout their studies, to support one another, share ideas and to develop good teamwork and collaboration skills. The same applies to preparation for an assessment, where working to develop a suitable approach or to gain a better understanding of the instructions could be improved by working together. However, there are caveats.

Firstly, remember that your peers might very well be wrong in their understanding. Do not take everything you hear from them as gospel, as so many students talk the talk, but fail when it comes down to the walk. Even "clever" students can get it wrong. If what your colleague is saying does not sound right, trust your instincts.

Secondly, avoid getting yourself into a muddle by listening to so many different ideas and interpretations that you get lost and confused. Keep going back to your own work, your own notes, and to the assessment guidance itself, as the primary sources of understanding. If there is confusion among your cohort, this is more likely a sign that your tutor has not communicated or clarified the instructions effectively. It is therefore right to ask the tutor to clarify any confusion for the cohort's benefit. (Remember, there is no such thing as a stupid question. If you are not sure on something, then it is always a good and valid question.)

Thirdly, answers or arguments developed by students are always better when they are that student's own. Too often we see papers where a student has clearly tried to emulate the ideas or approach of another student but have failed to properly encapsulate the issue or develop a persuasive argument around it. Your work needs to be your own and you will always make a much better paper if you develop the argument and build up the evidence entirely yourself. This is because a truly effective paper needs to have one central vision that sits at the heart of the argument: your vision.

Finally, it may be classed as plagiarism if there are signs of collusion between students. It depends on what your instructions are. For example, a group-based assignment may anticipate some copying if each student is submitting collectively developed work. However, in most cases, you need to make sure your work is your own to avoid any suspicions of academic dishonesty.

2. Understanding Assessment Criteria

Now we know how to understand what the instructions are asking us to do, it is worth taking a brief look at the assessment or marking criteria and the learning "outcomes" or "objectives" for your module.

Intended Learning Outcomes

Intended Learning "Outcomes" or "Objectives" (ILOs) are usually matched against a specific module and may even be further broken down into further detail against each specific class or lecture within that module. It is useful to read these, if only to have some understanding of what you are expected to learn on a module or take away from a specific class. It helps you identify the core issues that require closer attention (and notetaking), as well as helps you navigate and orient yourself through the different issues being covered. Perhaps most importantly of all, the ILOs should be crossmatched with your assessments for a module. As such, they provide excellent inspiration for understanding what you are being asked to evidence in assessments, as we are ultimately grading your achievement of those learning outcomes. This is why ILOs tend to get more complex as students move through their studies. A first year degree student might have ILOs like "be able to describe", "establish a persuasive argument with use of evidence", "conduct independent research", "weigh up different options", "perform standard calculus", and so forth. By the final year, ILOs would be more advanced, like "critically evaluate and assimilate a range of high-quality sources", "construct an evidenced and nuanced argument", "deconstruct and challenge existing evidence with use of quality research and critical analysis", "manipulate and assess large datasets to derive persuasive conclusions", and so forth.

Assessment Criteria

It is essential that you familiarize yourself with your assessment criteria on your degree or course. All courses should also have a set of Assessment Guidelines or Assessment Criteria. These tend to be more generic and apply across a range of modules. They may also be module-specific, which can be extremely helpful at deriving clearer understanding of your assessment expectations. Even your discipline-wide assessment criteria are essential reading. All marking carried out throughout your entire course should be in correspondence to these criteria. Markers refer to them frequently to make sure that we are consistent with our gradings and expectations across the cohort. Some criteria guidelines are better drafted than others. I have lost count of the amount of assessment criteria I've read that say unhelpful things like, "In terms of critical analysis, an excellent answer will demonstrate excellent critical analysis."

Usually, assessment guidelines will use specific descriptive terms depending on the grade boundary (e.g., moving from pass, to satisfactory, to good, to very good, to excellent, to exceptional). When providing feedback, we are often required to highlight to you the different elements that reached different boundaries (e.g., excellent communication and numeracy, but weak structure and analysis). As with ILOs, your assessment criteria will demand evidence of more challenging skills and knowledge as you progress through your course. You should familiarize yourself with your course's assessment guidelines and crossmatch your feedback against it. Furthermore, looking at expectations in boundaries *above* where you were scored will offer ideas of further steps to improve and reach those higher boundaries. For example, if you were graded as "competent" for "use of a range of materials", then you can explore what you need to evidence to achieve the grade boundary above (e.g., to score "good").

Key Assessment Criteria for Essays

While all degrees and courses will be evaluating a range of 'hard' and 'soft' skills amongst the cohort through a mixture of assessments, there is a common theme across courses around the world when it comes to assessing essays. In particular, essays will almost invariably be assessing a student's:

- Knowledge and Understanding
- Critical Analysis
- Application (sometimes)
- Answering of the Question
- Communication, Presentation and Structure
- Incorporation of Sources and Evidence

It is important to also be aware that these assessment criteria overlap and frequently interact. For example, a student with good knowledge and understanding will make use of appropriate and relevant sources. By contrast, a student with poor communication skills might fail to effectively execute a persuasive argument by critical analysis.

Knowledge and Understanding
Most modules will expect students to be able to demonstrate an understanding of the subject material, by showing both familiarity with and comprehension of the literature, debates and wider reading. A weak answer in this area will have important gaps (showing poor knowledge) or would make critical errors in explaining concepts and ideas (showing poor understanding). The very best way to improve your mark in this area is therefore to work hard at studying the materials and issues discussed throughout the course, as well as ensuring you follow the relevant reading. This does not necessarily mean detailed notetaking of *all* the reading, but the ability to dissect and pinpoint the key issues. It also means checking your understanding frequently and working hard to rectify areas of confusion or uncertainty.

If a student is struggling in this area, I always recommend that they seek out easier textbooks in the subject area. Most textbooks cover the same materials, but they vary in terms of their ease of use and accessibility. Some are better at breaking it down and simplifying it. Do not be afraid to refer to these "easier" sources when trying to understand a tricky subject: I do it all the time! From there, you can get the basic understanding, from which you can more easily begin adding deeper discussions and building on that knowledge.

There are other ways to check your understanding too. Many courses have consolidation work built in to help students check their understanding. Alternatively, many textbooks and revision guides have additional online resources that sometimes include multiple-choice tests. If you are really struggling, your tutor should also help you unravel areas of confusion if you utilize their office hours. There are also many online private tutors, who can provide you with 1-to-1 support in problem areas. For this, I recommend online tutor platforms, such as **Superprof, Wyzant** or **MyTutor**, or searching for helpful online courses on platforms such as **Coursera** and **Udemy** (see Chapter 12).

Just keep going and, most of all, keep reading. The more you explore a topic across a range of sources, the more you see it in different ways and with different examples, helping you to unlock it. However, be wary of over-confusing things. Sometimes things are much simpler than they sound, so do not be intimated by clever language and try to break things down or simplify them in a way that makes sense for you.

It is worth bearing in mind that understanding also speaks to the accuracy and conciseness with which you refer to different ideas and concepts. The more a student has understood a subject and read around it, the more enhanced is their ability to precisely explain a topic. It is one of the areas of essay tutoring which is hardest for me to tutor: I can tell you how to structure an essay, how to develop your critical analysis, where to find materials, and how to write effectively; but I cannot necessarily teach you how to improve your cognitive functioning. Nevertheless, it is fortunately an area that is quite easy to master. Academics are not looking to "trip you up" by setting essay topics on unfamiliar areas. 99% of the time we are focusing on the topics and issues that we have been teaching you in the classroom. Therefore, keeping generally engaged with your learning and taking the time to go back to the course materials will help significantly.

Analysis (or Critique, Dissection, Evaluation, Assessment, Appraisal, etc)
The importance of critical analysis to powerful essays is hard to overstate. It is one of the trickiest skills for students to master and it is perhaps the most essential skill if you are to shift from mediocre to superlative grades. Anybody can find or memorize relevant sources or arguments and just copy them into an essay or answer. That is relatively easy. What requires deeper intellect, understanding,

creativity and insight is the development of a persuasive critical argument that *builds on* those sources or studies.

Analysis is called for in all academic disciplines. In humanities and social science disciplines, it usually requires the construction of a persuasive argument or perspective based on existing materials and secondary sources. In STEM (science, technology, engineering and mathematics) disciplines, it can often refer to construction of persuasive findings based on evidence from both empirical research, application of processes and/or from a range of secondary sources (see Chapter 4 for more on these terms). The most important point, thus, is your ability to construct persuasive *arguments* on the basis of the evidence.

An essay that is jam-packed with relevant information, sources and correct explanations of the materials, but which does nothing with them, will never get more than a middle-level grade. A poor mark might also result from just listing all the pros and cons of a particular idea or proposal, as expected at pre-university level. These would be classed by your tutors as merely "descriptive" pieces of work, usually meriting a mid to lower range mark. By contrast, it is those pieces that *critique, question, manipulate* and *utilize* that evidence in order to construct an argument or reach a persuasive conclusion that will merit significantly higher marks.

You need to explain why a particular idea, theory or proposal is correct. You often do this by arguing why one half of the evidence is more persuasive than the other half: what evidence backs up the arguments in favour of your view and how can you challenge or undermine the conflicting evidence? It is this ability to unpick or explain away the opposing ideas, and move beyond just listing the pros and cons, that is essential to success. This is therefore expanded in the chapter that follows.

Answering the Question

"Answering the question" or "Following the brief" should hopefully be quite self-explanatory as an assessment criterion. It was also explored in detail in the first section of this chapter. It is worth stressing, however, that this is the essential component of *all* assessment criteria: they all go out the window if you do not properly follow the brief. Missing this criterion also implies significant weakness in understanding basic instructions, which is a fundamental attribute that any graduate must possess.

Many students make errors in this department. For example, if the instructions tell you to develop an argument, then make sure you develop an argument. If they say to refer to a specific source, then make sure you refer to that specific source. If they ask whether you agree or disagree, make sure you develop a reasoned argument that that sets out clearly whether you agree *or* disagree. If it is a problem scenario and is asking you to advise on a specific set of problems, make sure you advise on all the problems. And so on.

Communication and Structure

If you thought you could get through a degree without being a strong writer or communicator, possessing a good understanding of grammar, presentation and punctuation, then I'm afraid you thought wrong. Effective communication is the lifeblood of academia and it's one of the main assets that graduates of most disciplines should be able to evidence. Being able to write accurately and effectively, without any errors, typos or sloppiness, is a prerequisite for so many professions. During your studies you will therefore be required to work hard at perfecting clear, concise, accurate and effective communication. Poor communication diminishes a student's marks. It makes your work far less persuasive, makes it more difficult to follow and generally makes the reading experience unpleasant. Essential guidance on powerful and effective writing is therefore covered in Chapters 8, 9 and 11.

It is also hard to over-stress just how critically important effective structure is. It is no exaggeration to say that poor structure can very easily turn an excellent piece of work into a very poor piece of work, barely worthy of a pass. What many students (and even guidebooks!) do not realize is that structure is *so much more* than just having an introduction and conclusion. That is the easy bit, and it does not, by itself, produce higher grades. Structure in fact permeates your entire paper, right down to how you choose to structure your sentences and paragraphs, as well as your choice of section and paragraph topics. It's about having a clear, logical and coherent sequence to your work, where you are walking through the issues with an identifiable thread that is easy to navigate and follow. It is about your "academic voice", which commands the narrative and the subject matter throughout. The secrets of powerful and effective essay structure are detailed in Chapters 5 to 7.

Use of Sources
Academia is about research. Your lecturers and professors are likely to be world-leaders in research. Research is the heart and soul of academic life. What is more, it is an essentially important skill that academic courses aim to inculcate in all their students. Expectations in terms of your research skills will of course vary depending on the nature of the discipline and, more importantly, the stage of your degree or course (e.g., first year undergraduates will have less expectations than Masters' level students). That our expectations of you continue to grow over time shows just how important research skills are throughout your entire academic life.

Most academic courses will therefore include an assessment criterion which expects evidence of wider reading. In some cases, such as early in your degree, you may find that reference to the listed wider or non-essential reading provided through your course materials is sufficient. In reality, you are better served by going beyond this and demonstrating as much evidence of wider reading as you feasibly can, as soon as you can. Students have frequently asked me whether having lots of references and citations of wider reading will lift their mark. Or, conversely, whether a small amount is sufficient. As discussed in far greater detail in Chapter 4, you are likely better off adding more sources, rather than less, to your work.

Of course, use of sources can depend on the nature of the assessment. While research is often still required in assessments like exams, oral presentations and reflective writing, it is not usually expected to the same extent as when producing essays, reports, advice notes or dissertations. For example, in the former types of assessment, you will often need to show evidence of wider reading and point to key sources to inform your arguments, but you might not be cramming in as much as you can, such as with an essay or report. Your best bet is to make sure you read Chapter 4 in full, which contains much more detail on conducting effective research and the importance and skill of finding good quality sources.

Referencing
Curiously, referencing is an area that most students find particularly intimidating. I think a large part of this is a result of the way it is taught or explained (or, more accurately, *not* taught or explained) at many institutions. Referencing is incredibly important: it is an essential academic skill and goes to the heart of academic good practice. The good news, however, is that referencing is incredibly easy! As noted above, the more high-quality sources you have effectively integrated in your work, the better and more persuasive your work will be. By referencing those sources, you can signify to your tutors whenever you have located sources and woven these into your arguments. It also helps to delineate those points and ideas that are your own.

It does not seem to be the question of *when* to cite materials that students struggle with most; but *how*. The most important thing is just consistency in how you cite different materials, as well as conformity to any citation style you have been instructed to adopt. When given specific instructions to use a certain citation style (e.g., APA, Harvard, Chicago, etc), we are therefore also evaluating your ability to *follow instructions*. If you cannot refer to the guides on these methods and successfully adopt the instructions given, then it shows a weakness in this regard. All references are inherently simple to draft after you have read the explanations in Chapter 10.

Application or Advice

Application or advice could be a component within an essay, particularly in response to a problem scenario or a given set of facts. Application is slightly different to Analysis and overlaps in some ways with Knowledge and Understanding. It is generally premised on you applying principles, processes or rules to the particular set of facts and is therefore about showing an expert understanding of your subdiscipline's application *in practice*. For example, in law you may be applying legal rules to a set of facts (known as a 'problem question'), whereas in scientific disciplines you may be applying a code or process to a set of facts. In engineering, it may be applying certain equations and calculations to a dataset to evaluate a proposed solution.

Application requires you to have a precise and nuanced understanding of how rules, theories and codes could apply in practice, requiring you to show your "working" as you work through each of the steps and engage in accurate application throughout. You demonstrate this nuanced understanding by particularly identifying the pertinent or determinant facts that steer the conclusions being drawn, as well as identifying potential *grey* areas where the application is uncertain and either further information is needed or arguments in either direction need to be considered.

If it requires a written answer in an essay style answer, then it could be sensible to use IRAC (Issue-Rule-Application-Conclusion) structure when addressing a question requiring application or the provision of advice. This essentially means breaking down the problem into a series of issues or steps that need to be worked through methodically in turn (the 'Issues'). Working through each IRAC one at a time, you should follow the issue by explaining the *rule* that applies (e.g., in law this might be the relevant legal principle or statutory section, or, for science and technology, it might be a particular code, rule, algorithm, method or formula) (the 'Rule'). You should then engage in analysis and application of the rule(s) to that particular issue (Application), before ensuring that you clearly tie up the analysis on that issue with a conclusion ('Conclusion'). Your answer should therefore methodically work through a series of IRACs—in effect—where each 'issue' or step has the relevant principles and rules applied and concluded before moving on to the next. Your overall conclusion can then tie together your series of sub-conclusions.

3. Types of Essay

It is worth highlighting that there are also different essay *types*.

Narrative Essays
Narrative essays are focused on explaining things or telling a story from a personal perspective. They are predominantly experiential (based on experience or observation) and personal in tone. A common use for narrative essays is a "reflective essay", requiring students to engage in a deep, insightful and introspective reflection into a practical experience or their own learning journey. Reflective essays are an increasingly popular assessment method that can be found in small parts of many courses and programmes. They allow tutors to have a method of assessment for practical exercises (e.g., teamwork, debating, negotiating, etc) and, more importantly, they teach students important skills of

self-reflection and personal development. There is so much to be said on achieving excellence in reflective essays, with guidance provided in Chapter 9.

Descriptive Essays

Descriptive essays are commonly used in creative disciplines or the arts. The focus is on describing an event, object or subject with the use of descriptive, evocative, engaging, figurative or emotive language. It is like painting a picture with words and is about developing a student's art of expression and use of written language. As detailed in Chapter 3, many students struggle to recognize that the standard essay at university should not be "descriptive". Description should only be used as necessary to introduce or explain concepts that are essential to contextualizing the argument. In other words, only rarely will you be required to *just* "describe" in your essay. If it is a descriptive essay, this should be spelled out in the instructions.

Expository Essays

Expository essays are also quite rare and quite inconsistently defined. An expository essay focuses on *explaining* complex or specific information. The focus is on demonstrating understanding, as well as writing in a way that is appropriate for the target audience. There is an emphasis on balance and unbiased presentation of ideas, allowing the reader to absorb all the information. A how-to manual and most newspaper articles would be expository; they are not seeking to critically analyze or persuade, but rather to clearly lay out and explain the facts.

Argumentative Essays

The vast majority of essays at university level and beyond are *argumentative* essays. In the same vein as academic journal articles, such essays seek to *persuade* the reader of the essay's core position, argument or stance. They do this with the use of analysis, evidence and logic. Sometimes you can hear of other types of essay too, such as *cause-and-effect, compare-and-contrast* or *problem-methods-*

solutions essays, but really these are also just another form of argumentative essay: they require an argument relating to key *causes*, or a *compared* viewpoint, or potential *solutions* to an issue.

Most of the essays you experience will be argumentative essays and the focus is always on the argument. Understanding that your essay is seeking to persuade the reader of its conclusion, that is clearly set out early on in the paper, is something that most university students take some time to truly appreciate. Too many times I've asked a student finishing their paper, "So, what's your argument?" and they say, "Good question. I don't know." What is really being examined in an essay, in addition to all the criteria explained above, is the student's ability to produce a cogent and coherent argument that demonstrates good critical thinking and critical evaluation of the subject matter.

3. Your Argument

1. Critical Thinking

It has already been stressed just how important the development of critical analysis is. You will often hear this—or phrases such as "reading critically" or "critical argument"—in your studies. Many students are also hit with the disheartening remark that their work is "descriptive" in feedback: often shorthand for saying that it lacks critical engagement with the issues. It is thus essential that students work on their critical thinking skills and their ability to approach their studies and research with a highly analytical mindset. Compared to the other assessment criteria in Chapter 2, critical analysis is a more ambiguous expectation and one that many students struggle to grasp. That is the focus of this chapter.

When we talk about approaching your research "critically", we do not necessarily mean with a view to *disagreeing* with everything. It is really about *questioning* everything. We want you to engage with the debates and with conflicting ideas and theories, such that you immerse yourself amongst them and question their merit, reliability or persuasiveness. It is about developing your academic voice, where you do not necessarily take everything you read as truth, but instead develop a commanding grip on the nuances and uncertainties in your field. Academics love grey or ambiguous areas where issues are not clear and are open to differing interpretations. It is therefore about developing your skills of argumentation. Why is this view preferable to others? What evidence is there in favour of this view, as compared with a counter-perspective? What makes that author's theory or hypothesis more reliable than the alternative? Which aspects of this theory or idea appear more accurate and *why*? And so on.

I often therefore advise my students to question the conclusions and arguments of everything they read, even if propounded by a leading academic in the field or by someone they usually agree with. No one is right all the time and the beauty with academia is the openness to different ideas, interpretations and to contrary evidence. So, when we say "critical analysis", we could in fact be talking about any activity that goes beyond merely reading and repeating what has been said by others. It might entail things such as evaluation, appraisal, comparison, contrast, synthesis, examination, dissection, disputation, connection, testing, stripping or reframing of ideas. A failure to engage with your research critically would, by comparison, result in work that is merely a descriptive account. Just saying what others have said is descriptive. Just repeating the pros and cons, like with pre-university essays, is also descriptive. You need to then go further and explain which of the pros or cons are more powerful and persuasive and, most of all, *why*. Your essay is therefore not merely a report, describing the situation: it is fundamentally about seeking to *persuade the reader* of its findings and conclusions, with the use of evidence, rationality and analysis.

Look at the next passage and consider the balance of description versus analysis.

> *The United Kingdom (UK) is renowned for possessing an "uncodified" constitution where the rules are more disparate and consist of a combination of legal rules and non-legal or political conventions. Relying upon a strong foundation parliamentary sovereignty, it is also well-known for possessing a great amount of constitutional flexibility. As Jenkins has said, the British constitution 'is very amenable to change, having few or no special amending procedures.' Perhaps one of the more distinctive aspects of the UK's constitution is the reliance on uncodified and non-legal conventions, which continue to emerge, evolve and shape the British constitution through the ages. As Walker has argued, the UK constitution is in a constant state of 'unsettlement', where continuation and revolution regularly collide. Yet, whether the lack of codification is*

> a positive or negative aspect of constitutionalism, when compared with alternative 'codified' systems, remains open to debate.

Many students might consider that this is a rich and engaging passage, which would merit a strong grade. Indeed, it is well written, formatted, structured and shows good knowledge, understanding and use of materials and reading. However, if all the essay was written like this, it would not be capable of getting a distinction grade. Despite all that rich discussion, there is actually no analysis in that passage! It serves as a great introductory passage, to set the scene for the analysis coming up in the essay, but it alone does not provide the necessary evidence of analysis and argumentation skills.

By contrast, let's look at this passage in Nicholas Barber's article, *Laws and Constitutional Conventions* ([2009] LQR 294, 295):

> The first element of Dicey's claim, that courts will not, or cannot, recognize conventions, is plainly too broad. Courts can recognize anything they wish to recognize. Judges frequently make reference to dictionaries, encyclopaedias, and a host of other things. It would be surprising if they never recognized constitutional conventions. The interest in Dicey's claim lies in the difficult divide between recognition and enforcement, and the extent to which recognition can be equated with enforcement. [T]here are those occasions when the convention is indirectly enforced because of its connection with a distinct legal right. […] Courts indirectly enforce many things. A court faced with a tricky word in a statute might turn to a dictionary for clarification. In a sense, perhaps, the court then "enforces" this definition.

While I am not saying that this is an exemplary passage of academic writing, it illustrates my point perfectly. If you contrast this to the first passage, there is a far greater emphasis on *analysis*. It is questioning ideas, reframing them, and hypothesizing new ones. It is doing more than telling us information, it is seeking to persuade us about something to do with that information.

It is thus important to not just agree or disagree, but also to explain *why*. This is where you can evidence wider reading, knowledge and use of sources in order to deconstruct or dissect the hypothesis or idea in discussion. Is it backed up by data? Does it stand up to analytical scrutiny or are there holes or gaps in its logic? Do other academics or analyses disagree, and on what basis? Is it potentially biased? Is it outdated? Asking these questions when addressing ideas or theories in your essay's subject area will demonstrate fantastic critical thinking.

To strengthen your essay's emphasis on critical analysis over description, I suggest you always keep the following 4 A's in mind: Audience, Articles, Alternatives and Argument.

1) Think of the Audience

Imagining the reader—and having a sense of their knowledge, understanding and interests—is essential to getting the right balance between description and analysis. You need to imagine that your essay's reader is someone *intelligent and trained in your discipline, but unfamiliar with the intricacies of the specific subtopic under discussion*. Many students make the mistake of imagining that the reader is the equivalent of a peer or another student at their level. This then makes them "dumb down" much of the discussion and, instead of developing rich and engaging analysis of the critical issues in the field, they spend too much time defining and explaining basic concepts and ideas.

For example, if your discipline is law and the topic under discussion is negligence, you can assume the reader has a strong knowledge of law and legal principles, as well as a basic understanding of negligence, but will just need some brief explanation on the intricate or idiosyncratic elements of negligence. You therefore do not need to define what we mean by "statute", but you do need to concisely explain "duty of care". If your discipline is English Literature and the topic under discussion is Shakespeare's *King Lear*, you can assume the reader is well-read and has strong skills of literary interpretation but lacks specific knowledge on King Lear.

Intelligent readers, who are familiar with the discipline, will not be looking for a *description* of the issues. They are beyond that: they are instead looking for a rich, interesting, critical analysis of the subfield under focus. They not only need to understand it, but want engagement with the nuance, debates and discussions. A mistake you might make in such cases is to therefore engage in explaining basic ideas and concepts for the reader. Back to our Shakespeare example, a poor essay would begin explaining when and where Shakespeare was born, his development of writing in the early years, what other literature he produced, what King Lear is about and its plotline, and so forth, without any of this advancing the paper's central hypothesis. In fact, spending too long defining basic concepts and ideas does the *opposite* of making a student sound intelligent and knowledgeable. Explaining that Shakespeare was born in 1564 in Stratford-on-Avon would suggest that you think that knowledgeable English academics would not know when and where Shakespeare was born.

2) Think of the Articles

Important advice! Map your essays against academic journal articles in your discipline. It's a piece of advice I rarely see explained anywhere, much to my surprise. It's almost like a secret that tutors keep hidden from their students, waiting for them to work it out themselves. Peer-reviewed journal articles within your discipline are usually the gold standard of academic research in your field. When they are not teaching you, your tutors and professors will usually be writing or reading academic articles. Regardless of your discipline, we are teaching you skills of *academia* and giving you the skills to continue in academic study. This means evaluating your essay writing against the foremost essays in your field: the peer-reviewed journal article.

Go to your university's library or to Google Scholar and peruse critical articles on your subject. Make sure to focus particularly on those articles published in journals targeted at your discipline. It is extremely common to see articles covering a topic from a different disciplinary perspective, but the style, approach and rigour might be suited to readers trained from another discipline. If your discipline is Physics, for example, you might take note of articles in *Reviews of Modern Physics* or *Nature Physics*, but not something discussing physics in *Critical Arts Management*. If your discipline is Business Studies, you might pay closer attention to things like the *Academy of Management Journal* or *Journal of Business Ethics*, as opposed to management discourse in the *Journal of Sports Science*. Pay close attention to the critical reading your tutor refers to or includes as part of your course.

When you are reading such articles, look at the professional and objective tone, the reliance on evidence and analysis, and the advancement of ideas and arguments. You will notice that the authors are often *introducing* complex ideas and concepts concisely, but only to set the groundwork to advance the hypotheses of the paper. This all gives you a great sense of what academics in your field see as the gold standard of academic research. I feel that tutors are often grading university essays against their "publishability". With the grade adjusted to the level of the student (e.g., pre-university, undergraduate, postgraduate, PhD, and so on), very high grades could suggest the paper is close to being of a publishable standard or has the potential to be so. Grades closer to 100% at an advanced level in a degree might suggest that the paper is ready to be submitted to a journal.

3. Your Argument

3) Think of the Alternatives

When approaching everything around us critically, we are usually asking "Yes, but what if?" This means not just taking information at face value, but somehow challenging that information or questioning its veracity, accuracy, persuasiveness, effectiveness or relevance, and so on. In other words, we are becoming masters of the *alternative viewpoint*. This focus on the alternatives should inform your research, as well as the construction and development of analysis in your essay. Think about this in the context of Bloom's famous taxonomy of educational objectives, a version of which is reproduced below:

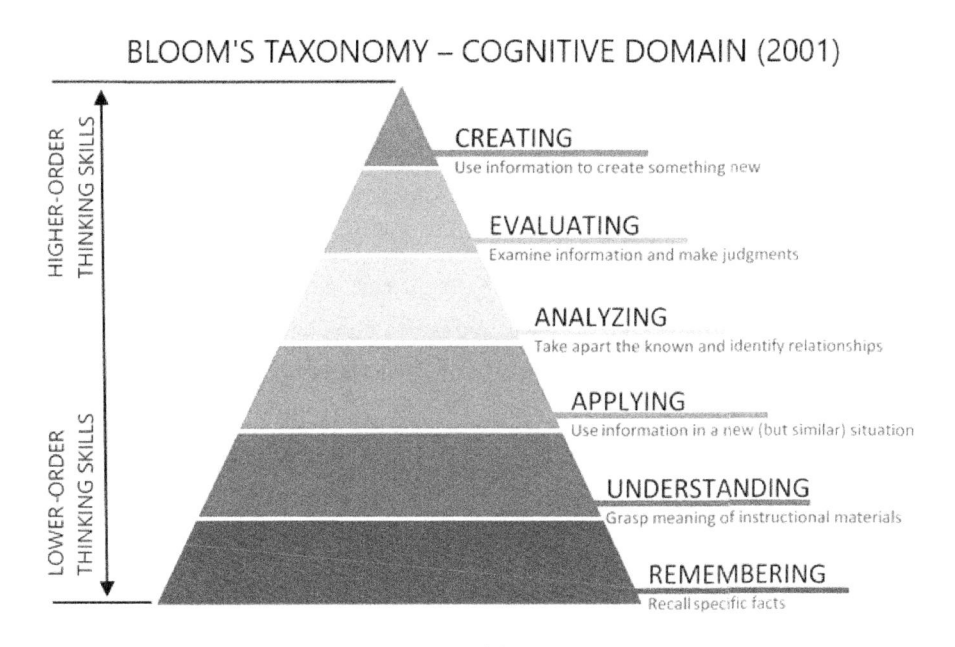

BLOOM'S TAXONOMY – COGNITIVE DOMAIN (2001)

HIGHER-ORDER THINKING SKILLS

- **CREATING** — Use information to create something new
- **EVALUATING** — Examine information and make judgments
- **ANALYZING** — Take apart the known and identify relationships
- **APPLYING** — Use information in a new (but similar) situation

LOWER-ORDER THINKING SKILLS

- **UNDERSTANDING** — Grasp meaning of instructional materials
- **REMEMBERING** — Recall specific facts

Bloom's Taxonomy
Image Credit: University of Florida

We academics still use Bloom's Taxonomy constantly as a tool to understand our students' learning journey and to "scaffold" your educational targets. We are ultimately aiming to develop those "higher order thinking skills" in our students.

In other words, not just the ability to understand and memorize information, but the ability to dissect it, evaluate it or even produce new ideas with it. When I speak of the focus on the *alternative viewpoint* in this section, it is these higher order skills I am referring to. It means not just learning the information, but questioning how that information can be deconstructed, critiqued or reconstructed. High quality essays are not about showing us you have understood or read something, they require you to show us that you are predominantly operating in these higher rungs of academic aptitude.

One way I like to explain it is to think of the mnemonic: "What?" → "Why?" → "What if?" This is ultimately the stages of depth and insight that could be applied to your essay's focus and we are actually looking for essays to spend *most of their time* on the "What if?". This means that you should not spend all your time explaining *what* something is; and you should not even use all your time explaining *why* it is like that; you need to solely use these contextual elements as the springboard to launch your focus on the "What if?". What if there was a different cause or pressure involved? What if this other academic's contrasting opinion is brought in? What if we apply the conflicting studies from recent research findings? What if we use an alternative method? What if we attempt to resolve the question with this proposed solution? What if this idea was cross-checked with the data? What if this dataset is faulty? What if this theory is circular or illogical?

This focus on the "What if?" also helps to remind us that being critical is not necessarily about poking holes and finding negatives. In many ways, we are looking for the best or optimum concept or solution, so are really focused on proposing better or more defensible alternatives. Just as an example, if your essay is arguing that the United Nations has failed as a concept, then instead of just being critical, you also want to introduce examples of *alternative* organizations, institutions or structures that could have fared better, evaluating their potential promise as an alternative.

What? → Why? → *What if?*

4) Think of the Argument

The most essential advice when it comes to striking the right balance between description and analysis is to make your *argument* the central theme of your entire essay. You should only include descriptive components that ultimately help to advance or clarify your central argument or proposition. When mapping out your essay and immersing yourself in its discussions, you should therefore always be asking yourself, "How is this advancing my argument?" If it's not, then it should probably be omitted. This is a fundamentally important practice that should help steer students away from going into lots of detail on interesting, engaging or "useful" information that does nothing to advance their argument. Such explanations or background information are not analytical nor critical, and they do not contribute to the theme and narrative of the paper, so they will only harm your grades, not help them. The only exception to this, of course, is if your assessment includes an instruction to specifically *explain*, *define*, *illustrate* or *describe* something specific. In such cases, you might need to dedicate some space to this. Otherwise, assume you can focus mostly on analytical discussions that are necessary to advance your argument.

In other words, you only need to explain or define something if it is necessary to give meaning to the argument. You also need to remember that the reader will have a general understanding of the discipline, if not the specific issue under discussion, so you do not need to define basic concepts and ideas. It is quite normal to include things initially within your essay and then later realize that it does nothing to advance the main proposition. It takes a good academic to spot this and then work out what can be omitted.

Focusing on the argument is also important to overall structure and narrative. If we are purely "critical" about everything and at every juncture, the paper will lack a direction of travel and clear flow. In addition to criticizing and questioning ideas and evidence, we should also be continuously moving forward towards the overarching proposition or hypothesis.

Writing Critically

I spend most of my time teaching university students to *unlearn* the approach to essay writing they learned in pre-university education. This approach, which is successfully drilled into young minds, leads to weak and ineffective essays at university level that lack critical analysis. For example, these essays will introduce the issue of the paper and invariably say that the "answer", between two alternatives, is "uncertain". They will then list all the pros and cons with the two competing ideas or potential answers. They then finally conclude by randomly plucking which side is preferable out of thin air, without having engaged in a focused discussion throughout of *why*.

At university level and beyond, you need to set out what your argument or findings are in the introduction and then dedicate the entire essay to *persuading* the reader of those findings. Instead of just listing pros and cons, you are critiquing them, questioning them, evaluating them, weighing them up, and so on. More detailed instructions on how to structure your essays is covered in Chapters 5-7.

In being critical, you also need to embrace nuance, ambiguity and the lack of certainty in any proposition or idea. It is hard to say that anything is 100% certain.

3. Your Argument

We could argue the sun won't rise tomorrow, that rabbits are aquatic animals, or that we all evolved from oranges. This recognition that all ideas are necessarily qualified should feed into the tone of your writing, where you want to be *cautious* or *qualified* in making any assertions. You can only be absolute when you can *prove* it, with reference to evidence, although this is rare. As such, you will often be using language such as "It could be deduced from this that", "This suggests that", or "It seems likely that" and so on. You are not saying something is 100% certain, because often this is hard to prove, but instead saying—from all the available evidence—it appears most likely.

Let's take some examples:

Too absolute
- *Communities can never govern internal issues efficiently.*
- *Anne Brontë was less talented than her sisters.*
- *Given that sound always travels at around 343m/s…*

Better
- *Communities **can often struggle** to govern internal issues efficiently (Pitman 2022).*
- ***According to estimates**, Anne Brontë's novels are not **as widely read** as her sisters' (Talbot 2020).*
- *Given that sound **usually** travels at around 343m/s, **when at ground level and in 20 degrees centigrade**, …*

You can see that we are moving away from subjective or opinion-driven language (e.g., that Anne Brontë was "less talented"), towards more objective, evidence-based language (i.e., that her books are "not as widely read"). The language is also more qualified and nuanced, recognizing there are exceptions to the rule and areas where certainty cannot be established. What is more, we are backing up statements with reference to evidence or data.

2. Making a Persuasive Argument

Using Analysis, Evidence and Reasoning

Having now established that your essay needs to be entirely focused on its core argument, it's worth examining how to make that argument more persuasive. This is a fundamental concept at the heart of an essay: good communication, structure, use of materials, elucidation of knowledge and referencing all serve to make the *argument* more persuasive. In many respects, therefore, this whole book provides guidance, tips and ideas on making your argument more persuasive and effective. In addition to this, there are three main overlapping tools we use when advancing effective arguments: evidence, analysis and reasoning.

The primary point is that you are basing your argument on the convincing and confident deductions you can draw from your analysis of the evidence. In other words, an argument is more persuasive when it has a logical or rational basis. For example, data or previous studies might back it up. Or we can see that its components are entirely logical or backed up by strong or more certain calculations and assumptions. If subject to scrutiny, we can see that the weaknesses in the argument are still outweighed by the strengths. We can point to matters with a high level of certainty, veracity or rationality that correlate accordingly. We can compare different causes and trace the likely source or key factors that have driven forward the result in question. In other words, we can draw upon a combination of evidence, analysis and reasoning to illustrate the strength or reliability of an assumption or idea.

Problematic Arguments
A really helpful way to illustrate this is to explore what makes a *weak* argument. I like to use an example of trying to persuade the reader that we need stronger

laws to deal with drink driving. In all cases, look for the potential weakness in the argument and consider how you might instead—with the use of better evidence, analysis or logic—make the argument more persuasive.

Arguments with no evidence	"Drink driving causes the biggest harm in our society. The government should therefore introduce stricter sentencing laws for it."
Circular arguments that just repeat the proposition	"To further protect society, the government should introduce stricter sentencing laws for drink driving. Doing this would benefit society by giving them better protection from drink driving."
Arguments based on faulty assumptions or understandings of causation	"Most drink drivers own a dog, so we should increase policing of drivers who own dogs in order to reduce the impact of drink driving."
Making propositions that are too severe or unrealistic	"Most drink driving offences are caused by males under the age of 30. As such, all men under the age of 30 should not be allowed to drive."
Making arguments that do not follow logically from the previous point (non sequiturs)	"The number of fatalities caused by speeding has increased over the past five years. As such, the government should introduce stricter laws on drink driving."
Arguments built off a lack of analysis or explanation of the data	"Road accident fatalities are growing year on year. Drink driving therefore needs stricter sentencing to help reduce these numbers."

Arguments based on appealing to emotion or subjective thoughts	"Drink driving can cause awful and unimaginably horrific injuries. It therefore merits the strictest level of sentencing possible."
Arguments based on overgeneralisations	"Everyone in society is impacted by drink driving. It therefore needs stricter sentencing."

Making Your Argument Persuasive

✓ **Use research and wider reading**

A student that demonstrates lots of knowledge and understanding of their subject field, with references to materials and resources, will inevitably be more persuasive. It demonstrates that their arguments and research are the product of rigorous engagement with different views, ideas, findings and perspectives. It also demonstrates that they are adept researchers and able to assimilate different ideas and hypotheses across the field. This inevitably makes their essays more persuasive. You can still get *your* views across using the evidence and ideas you obtain from elsewhere, because you can place greater prominence and credence on those ideas you find more persuasive.

✓ **Use analysis and reasoning**

Review the previous section and apply this to your handling of issues in your essay. Dissect or scrutinize ideas, findings and arguments from others. Play ideas off against each other (e.g., "Smith says this. However, Lopez persuasively argues that the better view might be..."). Use reasoning or logic to demonstrate why you are reaching these conclusions (e.g., "This is more persuasive because it takes account of the modern global context"). Doing this will produce a richer and more robust argument and one that is more clearly developed through critical engagement and deeper evaluation of the subject.

3. Your Argument

✓ **Look for the academic "debate" and get involved**

Essay topics are usually developed to feed nicely off existing academic debates and discussions. We love to set topics that will encourage you to "get involved" in an area with different ideas, perspectives and research foci. When approaching your argument, be on the lookout for these debates or areas of uncertainty, ambiguity or conflict within the literature. By offering a range of contrasting opinions or perspectives, they are fertile territory for you to develop your own argument or perspective.

✓ **Do not just focus on the pros, but why those pros are persuasive**

We have already said that just listing the pros and cons of a particular view, idea or approach is not sufficient. If you identify strong arguments that support your conclusions, then highlight what makes them "strong". As above, are those views widely accepted? Are they supported by robust research findings? Is their provenance (the source or individual behind them) reliable and reputable? Are the counterarguments against them weak?

✓ **Address the counterarguments**

Too often I see arguments that intentionally or inadvertently "ignore the elephant in the room". By this, I mean that the student never addresses the glaringly obvious criticisms that could be levied against their conclusions. *To be persuasive, you must not only explain why your findings are correct but address why those who would disagree with you are wrong.* When constructing your arguments, always listen to and address the imaginary critic. If someone was arguing against you, what would they poke holes in? Where would they say your conclusions are weak? What evidence would they use to undermine your findings? To be more robust and persuasive, you need to show that you have considered the views of these imaginary critics and that you can address or rebut their concerns.

For example, imagine your essay was arguing that a significant tax should be introduced on all businesses to help offset climate change. I would hope that this essay would, at some stage, deal with the economic risks and downsides of such an approach. Why would a government want to weaken its own industry in the global marketplace? This is a common elephant in the room I see when it comes to policy arguments, but the same principle applies in any discipline.

✓ **Use an appropriate methodology**
For some disciplines, such as in the arts and humanities, an effective methodology might simply be a critical analysis of the literature field. This might be sufficient to draw a persuasive and robust argument. In other cases, and certainly in scientific disciplines, you may be required to adopt a more hands-on methodology. For example, for a dissertation in a sciences discipline, you might be expected to undertake your own empirical study, along with a justification for your methodology or experiment design. Even in the social sciences and humanities, you might do well to carry out analysis on primary sources, rather than just secondary sources.

Just consider that your main aim is to establish findings and to persuade the reader of those findings. If going beyond what has been said by others and producing some analysis of primary materials is *absolutely necessary* to make you more persuasive, then consider how to do it. In most cases, however, it will not be necessary. You are probably able to persuade the reader just by building on existing materials and sources (see Chapter 4 on different source values).

✓ **Compare with peer-reviewed journal articles**
As mentioned, it amazes me how little this is explained to students. Your tutors are academics. Our work is usually premised on publishing our own papers in academic journals and we are training our students to walk in our footsteps. Academia is like a conveyor belt, where you progress through the stages: at the

start you are an undergraduate, then a postgrad, then a PhD candidate and, in the academic's mind, the end point is becoming a full-time *academic*. At least that is how you are pictured to us. To us, therefore, the gold standard of academic research is that which is published in internationally-renowned academic journals in our field and subject to rigorous peer review.

You should therefore picture the highly cited or influential papers in your discipline's field as outstanding "essays". Peruse articles in Google Scholar or your institution's library, considering things like structure, analysis, methodology and use of sources. Not all highly cited papers are "essays". Some are simply monologues, summaries, notes or reviews that have become successful. In fact, university essays can be even more rigorous than published papers, as we expect detailed evidence and analysis to be compressed into a small word count. Still, your tutor is likely to be marking your essays against their "publishable" qualities.

✓ **Use concise writing**

You might be reading all of this and thinking, "But, how on earth can I fit all of this into just 2,000 words!?" And you are quite right! It's incredibly difficult to make an outstanding essay within the short word count we impose upon you. That is a big part of the challenge. It is often rightly said that it is harder to write fewer words than more. Most people write by getting it all out and then have the task of pruning it back and cutting things away, so that they can fit it all in. It is a challenge. However, going through this process of pruning and refining makes for a much richer and more engaging essay, where every word counts, and all the points are well-constructed. Read Chapter 9, which includes loads of detailed tips and guidance on achieving more concise writing.

3. Forming an Argument

Given that the heart of an incredible essay is the elucidation of an *argument*, what is your argument going to be? Many essay instructions will give you a clue as to where you should focus your argument. These are known as *closed* essay questions, where your argument needs to fit into the narrowly prescribed focus of the question. For example, if your instructions ask you to "agree or disagree", then you *must* ensure that your argument clearly sets out its position. Similarly, if asked to "compare" or "contrast", then you are usually being asked to produce an argument as to which of the options is more accurate, reliable or persuasive. You cannot form an argument that does not relate in some way to a comparison or contrast of the two.

By contrast, sometimes instructions are more open-ended or ambiguous in their requirements, such as saying "critically discuss". These are sometimes referred to as *open* essay questions, where they leave you far greater latitude in terms of choosing ideas or views you want to promote in your paper. It is important to be aware of this distinction when it comes to determining what your argument is going to be. If it seems quite narrowly restricted by the question, then make sure you focus on those parameters or provide a view on that specific matter.

That said, even in such "closed" essay questions, you can still *both* answer the question *and* extend an interesting overall argument or perspective *as well*. This does require powerful and concise writing, as well as highly effective structure, to effectively incorporate both an answer and a broader argument together in a clear manner. However, it makes for a far more impressive, powerful and engaging response to the question. For example, if the instructions ask you whether you agree or disagree that school education should only cover science and technology and not teach arts and humanities, a good answer might not only persuasively and comprehensively "disagree" with the premise, but also advance a view that technology will allow for a better combined education of arts and science.

3. Your Argument

Some further tips:

✓ **Immerse yourself in the topic**

When you first come to read the essay instructions, you are very unlikely to have a view on the subject matter or issue. That is totally normal. Your view will only begin to emerge once you truly immerse yourself in the topic in that 'Foundational' step (see Chapter 1). Identify the subjects of the essay (as discussed in Chapter 2) and start doing plenty of reading around them. As also noted there, you want to read the essay instructions as early as possible. The more you become aware of the different research, ideas, debates, concepts and theories in the subject area, the more you will start to form your own views and will be eager to express them. Much more advice is given on research in Chapter 4.

✓ **Keep focused on the assignment instructions when formulating an argument**

While it is important you get "immersed" in the research field and start to grapple with differing ideas, concepts, data and approaches, it is also important to remain tethered to the specific instructions in the assignment brief. It is very easy to start latching onto interesting ideas and concepts but losing focus on what the essay has asked you to concentrate on. The need to keep going back to the brief was discussed in Chapter 2.

✓ **Read critically**

This chapter has discussed you taking a generally "critical" approach to your research and essay planning. Ultimately, this critical engagement with everything you read is about you developing yourself as an authority on the essay's subject and beginning to develop your academic voice within it. You cannot expect to know everything. I often say that the more you research, the more you realize how little you have learned. At least that is how it feels. However, the reality is that *you are* developing knowledge and understanding, as well as a command of the key themes, concepts and ideas, as you critically engage with the subject matter.

✓ **Pay close attention to course materials**
Essay topics are rarely on subjects that have not been covered in the course, either extensively or briefly. You must make sure that you identify all the materials in your module—be it teaching, reading, guidance, notes, lectures, and so on—that have touched on or addressed the niche of the essay topic. These will usually give important clues to the kinds of issues that might be relevant in the debate or subfield, as well as potential ideas on the different views or approaches one might bring to them. This also helps you to remain on topic and hit the brief.

✓ **Locate the ideas you agree with and then find the evidence to support them**
As you conduct your research and critical reading for the essay, you will begin to get a sense of the views and ideas you agree with (in the 'Focusing' step). Start asking yourself, which ones do you find persuasive and why? Which ones can be supported or subject to criticism? What evidence supports a particular view or idea? Do not worry if your views and opinions change as your essay progresses. You may later discover further evidence in favour of the counter-perspective or simply begin to change your mind. This is fine and is the natural result of research and development of your expertise. None of the existing work you have done will be wasted.

✓ **Try brainstorming**
Many students find it helpful to put pen to paper and to begin drawing spider diagrams on the essay subject matter. You can Google the process of doing this if you think it might be helpful to you. In general, you want to write whatever is the primary subject in the middle and then begin linking off to other bubbles that contain subcategories of information. These bubbles can also link off yet further

to smaller bubbles or can be linked together. You can also express information about the link by titling or adding information to the line between bubbles. In some ways, it might look like this:

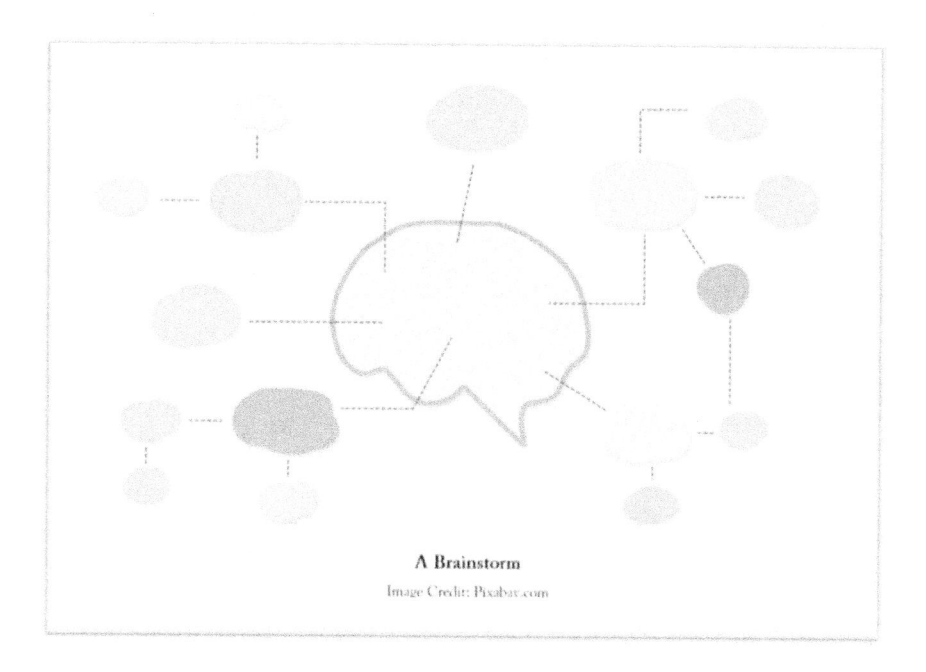

A Brainstorm
Image Credit: Pixabay.com

Having put this all together, you can then get a sense of connections, links and overall themes. This could help start to visualize a way forward, which ultimately provides the direction and focus for your argument.

✓ **Your conclusions do not have to be absolute**
It is perfectly acceptable to draw a view which supports some elements of an idea but rejects others. For example, even if your instructions say to "agree or disagree" with an idea, it is perfectly okay to develop an argument that "broadly agrees but recognizes these problems." It is really about having a view—whatever that view is—and backing it up with analysis and evidence constructed into a persuasive argument.

How to Write Amazing Essays

- ✓ **Do not worry if the argument you make is "right"**

In many ways, any argument is right provided it is backed up by evidence. Your tutor is not necessarily looking for you to agree with them or to simply agree with what you have read. The important factor here, however, is to make sure that any arguments you do make are backed up by persuasive and powerful evidence and analysis. Be careful not to disagree with literally everything you cover, including well-established ideas, just for the sake of appearing critical.

- ✓ **Do not worry about being ground-breaking**

Many students put themselves under pressure to come up with a super clever or ground-breaking argument. This is not necessary. All you need is to put *your own slant or perspective* on the issues being explored. This point is discussed further in the next section on developing your own essay topics.

4. Developing Your Own Essay Topic

Later in their academic studies and beyond undergraduate level, students are increasingly expected to develop their own essay topics. In your final year at undergraduate, you are likely to be required or encouraged to undertake a dissertation, which will require you to formulate your own research question. At postgraduate level, developing your own research questions is standard. Even early in your studies, you may be faced with very broad "open" questions that give you considerable latitude in developing the essay topic. In such cases, many students often struggle to identify a suitable subject area or to generate a suitable question or argument they want their thesis to pursue. Here are some super handy tips to help:

- ✓ **Focus on your interests**

It might seem obvious, but it is surprising how many students lose sight of this. So many students try to pursue an idea that sounds clever or impressive, or that caters to the interests of their tutor, without thinking about their *own* passions and interests. Essays are always so much more exciting and interesting, and usually better quality, if the student is interested in the subject. Moreover, you will find the process more enjoyable and are likely to maintain engagement if the topic interests you. You can think creatively too. If your passion is dogs, cars or crime dramas, then think of an essay topic in your field that will link to dogs, cars or crime dramas. There is usually a way! Relatedly, try to find an area that you feel confident in. Do not take on a clever topic just to sound clever unless you truly understand it. Some areas within your discipline will be more comfortable for you than others: do not make your work harder than it needs to be.

✓ "Just keep reading."

Maybe you have a rough idea of an area that interests you, but you are struggling to formulate a research question. This is a very common situation. When I was producing my Master's dissertation, I had the same issue, and I will never forget the advice that my supervisor gave me: "Just keep reading." It worked! The more you read and uncover on the general subject matter, the deeper and richer your insights and thoughts will be. You will begin to identify ideas or arguments that interest you, that can be critiqued, or that can be subject to engaging discussion and analysis. Your understanding of the field will become more nuanced and you will gradually develop further ideas and greater authority.

✓ **Choose a topic with a Goldilocks volume of existing literature**

You are looking for a nice volume of existing research on the subject: not too much, not too little. If there are fewer materials to draw upon, it makes your research and the development of ideas difficult. It means you are stuck with writing largely from conjecture and without being able to refer to materials and evidence in constructing your argument. It might also make it difficult to develop interesting ideas or to formulate a good thesis topic. By contrast, if there is too much existing research, you are likely to feel overwhelmed and are at risk of missing key concepts or themes that should have been identified and properly examined. If the literature field feels too broad, then you could keep narrowing your topic focus, going deeper into a particular aspect within that field.

✓ **Do not worry about being ground-breaking**
As noted above, many students put themselves under pressure to come up with an idea that is genius or ground-breaking within the subject. At undergraduate and Master's level, you really do not need to do this. Even at PhD level, your contribution to knowledge need not be ground-breaking or shift the paradigm of the field into a different dimension. So do not worry if your topic argument aligns closely with the ideas of others: you do not need to 'reinvent the wheel' and try to change the field. You can simply put your own critical thoughts and perspectives upon the existing field. Likewise, if doing empirical or primary research, just keep it simple and adopt a methodology that is tried-and-tested.

However, as a final note, you still need to demonstrate *independent* critical thought in your argument. Do not argue something that is so obvious because there will be no real debate. For example, do not have a main argument like "urgent action is needed to address climate change"—well duh! I see arguments like this a lot and I am usually waiting for the critical issues to be explored, but because the argument is so routine and lacks meaty opposition, the critical issues just cannot be brought in. The better approach if you want to make this argument is to use that as the baseline and then advance a *further* argument from here. For example, arguing that a global fund should be created to invest in renewable energy infrastructure. This is something that could at least be debated and compared to alternative options to address climate change.

✓ **Do not do empirical work unless it is truly necessary**
By empirical work, we are talking about you conducting your own primary research, such as interviewing subjects, experimenting with samples or conducting data analysis, and so on. Usually this will require a series of steps to

follow at your institution, including rigorous ethical approval or health and safety checks. In some disciplines, particularly from a sciences field, carrying out primary research might be required or expected. In many other fields, it is presented as an option. The same applies here in terms of trying not to be 'ground-breaking'. In my field of law, students have frequently asked me whether they should do empirical research for their dissertation, believing it would strengthen their chances of getting a high grade. My answer is almost always *no*. It requires a huge amount of work and effort, with a lot of formalities to be followed. The findings from a short study are likely to be superficial and you are unlikely to have enough time to engage critically with the context of your research in the field. As mentioned above, however, a lot is discipline-dependent. But only consider it if it is absolutely necessary to achieve your argument and if you have a clear methodology which is going to be quick, simple and painless.

✓ **Be prepared for your arguments or topic to change — and do not worry if they do**

Research is an organic process and it necessarily must be. Nobody should pursue a research question or seek to promote an idea without a willingness to be persuaded otherwise. Indeed, that is a core aspect of critical thinking: a willingness to critique your own ideas and to recognize differing views and perspectives. We know this as supervisors and tutors, and so we anticipate that research ideas will evolve and change to some extent. However, if you can, try to evolve them in a direction that captures much of your existing research and notes, so that you can maximize these.

✓ **Do not just look for problems, but also for solutions**

An essay which just focuses on persuasively proving or disproving an idea has value. One that both disproves something *and* promotes a better solution or understanding is superior.

- ✓ **Determine if a case study approach might work**

If you are in a literature field with too much going on or you are struggling to identify a focal point within your field, consider taking a 'case study' approach in your thesis. By this I mean choosing specific real examples or stories which can be subject to more rigorous analysis *in the context* of the subject, to provide further insights and thoughts. You still need to enrich your dissertation with analysis of existing literature, but it might help give you a focal point and give you plenty to talk about. Just as an example, I was recently supporting a student who wanted to look at global financial crime and corporate governance. Her ideas were too broad and fragmented. I proposed she look at the Wirecard scandal, recently across the news, as compared with the Enron scandal and—*voila!*—she had clear focus.

4. Research

1. Embracing the Researcher Lifestyle

As should be abundantly clear from the last chapter, an outstanding essay is the product of excellent research. You cannot attain top grades at university without developing the skills of efficient and effective research. This chapter is therefore jam-packed with key tips and hints on becoming an efficient and effective researcher.

Being a researcher is *wonderful*. It's time to forget any worries or concerns you might have about spending lots of time conducting research for your essay. Change your mindset, if you haven't already, to recognize that research is one of the most enjoyable, interesting and relaxing jobs out there. When I was doing research on my undergraduate, Master's and PhD dissertations, I would often reflect on what I was doing with my day, compared to what the average worker. The average worker would be stuck in a hot and stuffy office, clocking in for their boss, kowtowing to their boss's demands, juggling multiple overwhelming tasks, and continually under pressure to hit unceasing deadlines. They would leave home early and then get home late, with a lot of commuting in-between.

My day? I would take my time and walk everywhere with a leisurely pace. If it was sunny, I was studying in the garden, in a park or at the beach. I would join my friends for lunch or would finish early if there were social plans. I would take regular coffee breaks from the library or my desk, where I might sometimes sit and enjoy a book with my croissant. I would have plenty of time to go to the gym and play sports. I would manage my own workload and would know best what jobs would be better for me, depending on my mood. I would all the while be thinking of interesting ideas or reading about interesting things. It's a wonderful lifestyle!

So, I call on you to recognize that there are not many jobs more pleasurable, engaging and relaxing than being a researcher. It is of course important to remain focused, disciplined and to build in routines. But if you compare relaxing in the library with a book to that future high-flying career you are aspiring to, you will realize that getting up and going to "work" as a researcher is easier by comparison.

Believe it or not, research can be *fun* when you get into it. If your research ideas and arguments develop, and your confidence in your niche slowly grows, you can begin to get excited by the structure and direction of your paper. In many ways, it can also be something of a treasure hunt. You are dedicated to writing a persuasive thesis on a topic and, in doing that, you want to locate all the evidence and materials you can use to achieve that. Oh, the excitement when you find a quote in a book or a study referenced in a journal that backs up a key point you are trying to make!

Research is a huge part of any great essay. You should be spending most of your time researching. The writing and formatting part comes together so much more easily when you have done proper research. Especially when you have lots of notes and lots you are eager to talk about. The rest of the chapter therefore gives lots of hints and tips on producing effective research in an efficient manner, st your researcher lifestyle more generally.

✓ **Develop healthy and sustainable routines that work for you**

Build routines that include lots of dedicated research time into your working week. Treat your academic study like a self-employed job—and a wonderful one. Make sure your routine is healthy and sustainable. Do not overstretch or place unbearable demands on yourself. Your routine needs to be manageable and enjoyable. However, make sure you do get up in the morning, drink a coffee (if that is your thing), and do your "getting ready for work routine", just as you would for a job. Research is also flexible as a job, so you can make your routine work for you. If you go to the gym in the morning, then you can start slightly later and finish slightly later. If you are definitely a night owl, then you can start later in the day. If certain weekdays are used for leisure, swap them with a weekend day. Make your working week your own. As long as you work in plenty of focused research time when you are at your most productive and maintain a healthy balance, then you should be fine.

✓ Utilize and enjoy different working environments

Research can be a wonderfully flexible lifestyle. Instead of being stuck in one place, you can do it anywhere and at any time. If it's a nice day, go and study on the beach or in a park. Go for a coffee in a café and study there. If you have access to the university's physical library or a local library, make use of it. Maybe see it as your place of work. Or, simply, work at your home desk, sometimes on your bed, sometimes on the couch. Whatever it is, you have a wonderful opportunity to enjoy different working environments. It helps keep you stimulated and makes your working day varied. The same applies in terms of the media you are using. Borrow physical books from the library if you can, to mix up the style of media you are engaging with. Use a Kindle, which does not emit blue light. I did research on holiday in Croatia with my Kindle. I have even done research sitting in my car with a book.

✓ Take regular breaks

It's a cliché now, but it's so important. Maybe you are a homebird, who only wants to work in their home office. That is fine. Either way, make sure to work in lots of breaks. Far from wasting time, taking frequent breaks helps boost your concentration, cognitive functions and longevity, while also improving mood. If you are using the screen a lot, take a break with little to no screen time. Make sure to rest your eyes, such as focusing on objects far away. If you are getting little fresh air, take a walk or just sit in the garden listening to the birds. Your breaks want to be little and often, with plenty of longer breaks worked in, such as for lunch or to do another activity.

✓ Fill up your spare hours in the working week with research time

If you are in a period of rest or leave, with the ability to focus on your academic study full time, then researching your essay should be your full-time job. If, as with many people, you are juggling your essay research with other demands—be it other assignments, work, childcare, or anything else—then fill up spare space you have with research time. As mentioned, research can be a more relaxing and enjoyable task than most others you will face in your work. It can be a useful reprieve from your other work. Enjoy "taking a break" from other things by getting out your book and resuming your immersion in your field and your treasure hunting.

✓ Control distractions

Distractions are a normal part of life. I am always facing distractions in my work. Common ones are clicking onto social media, the news, your emails, or friends and family. Other ones could be phone calls or friends who are always trying to get you to drop your work and join them at the bar. Take action to take control of these. It is surprisingly empowering to install a blocker on your browser or phone to restrict your use of social media, even if only to act as a reminder that now is "work time". Similarly, it is empowering to put your phone on to vibrate and to only answer repeated calls (i.e., emergencies). It is great to take a break and join friends sometimes. Being an academic now, you are now free to do that. However, see it more as a reward following a long stretch of work or simply tell your friends you will join them later or another time. You are at work.

✓ Build in rewards

Relatedly, to make research enjoyable, build in plenty of rewards. Taking a break and having a refreshing drink can be a reward. Going for a coffee or joining friends for lunch can be a reward. Watching half an hour of TV or TikTok can be a reward. Going out in the evening can be a reward.

✓ **Keep well in mind, body and spirit**
We often hear the phrase "healthy body, healthy mind". There is a lot of truth in this. Keeping fit and active helps improve your focus, energy and concentration. For some this might be going to the gym or playing sport, for others it might be taking a walk or having a swim in the river. The same applies in terms of diet. Eating and drinking well will improve your body's chemical balance and will improve your mood and focus. You might do well to consume plenty of brain foods and lots of antioxidants, as well as making sure you keep hydrated with water. But still treat yourself (as one of your rewards) occasionally. Your spirit and mood are equally important. Some practice mindfulness or meditation, others pray or observe their faith, while some join a club or play sudoku. Whatever helps you relax is good for you.

✓ **Do not be worried if you are having a bad day**
It's a simple fact: some days we are firing, and our brain is fully focused and on form. On other days we are just not there. Maybe it's late and you are tired. Maybe you have got something on your mind that you cannot ignore. Do not worry. This is the advantage of being "self-employed" as an academic. Call it a day early, get some rest, and come back when you are on better form. You will do far better and more efficient work when you are rested, so you will probably be *more* productive by stopping and making sure you come back to it the next morning. Alternatively, move to a less mind-consuming task. For example, start mapping out your essay plan and moving the pieces around or looking for more sources for analysis the next day. Alternatively, complete more menial tasks on your to-do list and clear the decks for work the next day.

✓ Take advantage if you are on form

On the flipside of the previous point, take advantage of those times when you are on form or making rapid progress. Maybe stay on that additional couple of hours in the library if you are rapidly producing lots of notes and do not want to break up the flow. You can have a lie-in or take a longer lunch tomorrow, as a reward, if you capitalize on this moment when you are making great headway.

✓ Just get started

I know this is one of those "Well, duh!" statements. Usually followed by, "It's not that easy." And it's true. It is very easy to start the morning by procrastinating and stretching out time on menial things, while reducing the time available for more pressing things. However, try getting your research notes straight back out, loading up the next document and resuming your reading in the first moment you sit at your desk. As you know, getting started is the hardest bit, but it gets far easier from there. As soon as you are reading your notes again or writing again, you will realize it is really not that bad! If it helps, I find that starting by reading back through the last few pages of whatever you were last working on can help kick the brain cogs back into gear.

✓ Find your own best practices

You know best how you work best. That is the beauty of being your own boss as an academic researcher. You can use whatever techniques, practices or routines are best for you. You can continually reflect on what has or has not worked, so that you can continually improve your own working practices. I am still improving mine! I know professors of thirty years who are experimenting with different working routines. We are all learning how to do our best work and that is one of the joys of being an academic.

2. The Source Hierarchy
Source Value

Not all research sources are created equal. Your tutor will be marking your work evaluating both the relevance, breadth and depth of sources you use, as well as their *quality*. This is an important thing to consider because, these days, so many students think they can conduct "research" by just doing lots of Googling. If that is all you do, then that is weak research. Your discipline will have expectations about what a quality source would look like, but it is likely to be a peer-reviewed article, a monograph (a single authored book written by an academic) or a chapter in an edited volume (an academic book with multiple authors writing different chapters). By contrast, a weak source would be an online blog or some other website with little provenance or reliability. In other words, there is a hierarchy of value in different sources. You should prioritize reading and referencing 'higher quality' sources—in other words, academic articles and books—to attain higher grades. Of course, different disciplines might ascribe slightly different values to sources. For example, in my traditional discipline of law, students can also see legal sources, such as case law and statute, as key primary sources with high value. Take note of the types of sources that are likely to be valued in your field. This is rarely going to be sources you can find by just searching with Google.

Primary Sources

Academic Articles and Books

Textbooks

Official Publications and Documents

Newspapers and Periodicals

Reputable Blogs

Blogs

The Academic Source Hierarchy
Image Credit: Author's Own

I place *primary sources* at the top of this list. These are the original sources, whereas the other sources listed represent 'secondary sources', i.e., analysis upon primary sources. What is a primary source depends on your discipline. As mentioned, in law, it would be the law! In languages or in English literature, it might be the poem or novel under focus. In history, it might be a record or document from an archive. In a scientific discipline, it might be empirical research or an experiment you have carried out. If you are carrying out analysis of a primary source, you are going straight to the source and putting your own interpretation upon it. There is no reason why anyone else's interpretation is better than your own, so your analysis and evaluation of it carries considerable value.

Next in priority is *academic articles and books*. Do a search in your institution's library, on Google Scholar, or on databases like JSTOR, SSRN or Science Direct, to find examples of these. Academic journals in your field will also all carry a different value themselves. In my field, for example, the Cambridge Law Journal carries much greater value than the Oxford University Undergraduate Law Journal. Not least because the former is edited by and has articles written by leading academics, whereas the latter is edited and written by undergraduate students. This is not to say that these lower-ranked journals should never be cited in your work, but that they are going to be seen in a more critical light than references to more reputable sources. A good tip can be to use these less reputable sources to find links to higher value sources: the student's article is likely to refer to leading authorities and papers in the field.

Peer-reviewed journal articles are considered valuable in academic research because, in order to be accepted for publication, a submission is subject to review by authorities in that discipline. Academic books—including monographs and edited volumes—can be equally valuable for the same reason. These will have their own scrutiny process, with academics evaluating the final manuscript and checking the veracity and accuracy of their arguments. Indeed, even the publisher of books can also be a relevant factor: there is a big difference between Hart or Oxford University Press with, say, the East Cornwall Fun Factory Press.

Textbooks are slightly different to monographs. Whereas monographs tend to be highly analytical theses, dedicated to detailed scrutiny of niche or complex subject matter, textbooks tend to be much broader and lighter touch. They are more focused on explaining or simplifying a subject. Nevertheless, textbooks can vary in value. A short revision guide from an unknown independent publisher will not have the same value as a widely cited and recognized compendium, published by a leading academic publisher, and written by a renowned expert in the field. What is more, just as with monographs, textbooks can contribute to knowledge and be useful sources of ideas and existing research in your field. As such, this level can also include online directories or information resources where these are exclusively written and edited by experts, academics or practitioners in your field.

Next is *official publications*, reports and documents. For example, a report published by an authoritative consortium (e.g., Intergovernmental Panel on Climate Change), an international institution (e.g., United Nations or European Union), or by a government body (e.g., the Department of Health), is likely to carry significant weight and value. This could also include publications from reputable organizations or consortia within your field. For example, if looking at humanitarian aid, then publications from the Red Cross or Oxfam will carry great value; if conservation, the WWF or Greenpeace's publications will be powerful sources.

Newspapers and periodicals can certainly carry value as academic sources. Once again, they can vary in terms of their provenance and reliability. For example, in the UK, you would be better served referencing The Times, The Guardian, The Telegraph, The Independent or BBC News, as opposed to a tabloid newspaper or a local periodical. The same applies for periodicals such as magazines, with many reputable magazines—e.g., Science, The Economist, Scientific American, National Geographic—carrying greater value than a lesser-known, independent ezine. Of course, something to be aware of is that many media publications have a political bias, particularly newspapers or political magazines. What is more, while articles are edited, journalistic writing can be less rigorous, more headline-focused and sometimes written by laypersons in the subject.

Then we have *reputable blogs* and online media. There are likely to be many blogs written by (and/or edited by) reputable academics or practitioners in your field. I would probably add to this rung a collection of other valued yet less reliable sources, such as working papers, PhD or Masters theses, or unpublished manuscripts. These can have significant value, especially if written by a subject matter expert, but they have each not been subject to full peer review.

Then we come to *blogs*. I say blogs, but really this is shorthand for anything random you can find on the internet which is not any of the above. Many of these sources have so little value that you are better off leaving them out than in! A common one here is "essay mill" websites that charge students huge sums of money to churn out rubbish essays for them, usually thrashed out in a few hours by a less-experienced graduate. Many of these sites publish samples of their essays or run Google-optimized blogs to attract traffic and most of these essays are literally trash. So do not cite random sources like www.essays4u.net or www.johnnysmusings.co.uk (both made up). Another well-known culprit here is, of course, Wikipedia. Wikipedia is an excellent *resource*. But it is not a source. Use it solely to locate source material or for inspiration and never use it as your main research database.

So how do you use this pyramid? Well, as you can guess, you want to try and evidence your arguments and conclusions making use of *as many higher value sources as possible*. If you can find evidence in a working paper, newspaper or a Master's thesis, then see if these link to a better higher value source you can use instead. Or simply search for a higher value source that expresses or evidences the same point. However, if these really are the *only* available evidence for that point, then use them. For example, I would cite newspapers as evidence of a real-life event occurring because this is unlikely to be better expressed or explained in any of the other sources. I would not cite a newspaper in relation to a theory in my academic discipline. I would cite a PhD thesis if it is covering points or ideas that are well encapsulated and have not been covered better in an academic article. And so on.

Source Relevance and Reliability

The source hierarchy categorizes the value of different *types* of source, but what about the relevance and reliability of the source itself? For this, it helpful to consider the PROMPT criteria developed by The Open University and explained below. PROMPT stands for Presentation, Relevance, Objectivity, Method, Provenance and Timeliness. While you may not need to rigorously check every source against these criteria, it is a useful list of general considerations when appraising different sources.

Presentation

While poor and shoddy writing might not necessarily mean the underlying information is poor, it is usually an indicator of poor production. A source published by a reputable organization or subject to rigorous scrutiny is likely to have been proofread and edited thoroughly. A blog bashed out by someone with little subject matter expertise might contain typos, grammatical errors, inconsistent formatting or poor structuring. Poor presentation can also negatively impact your ability to accurately decipher the information included within a source. While I have highlighted peer-reviewed articles as being examples of high standard essays, I have seen many peer-reviewed articles that have atrocious structuring or planning, and where it is hard to understand the author's meaning.

Relevance

Is the source relevant to your area of inquiry? Perhaps it is focused on subjects or areas that are not entirely relevant or linked. Perhaps it is too specialized or too general. Sometimes you are looking for small kernels that carry relevance within a large piece of work. In which case, read the handy guidance below on efficient research skills.

Objectivity

Most academic work should ideally be conducted from an objective and dispassionate viewpoint, although this is not always the case. A common situation is that an author is determined to prove their viewpoint such that they omit contrary evidence or interpret data in a slanted manner. Reading critically, as discussed in Chapter 3, will help you to try and spot this. It might also be that the author or publication has a particular political leaning. A common way to spot this would be when they use sensationalist or emotive language. Look at newspaper articles, for example. They are usually focused on generating shock or intrigue, such that they frequently resort to emotive language. Having strong opinions in academia is of course a good thing, as long as you recognize them for what they are and rationalize them effectively. Having passionate views—as long as they are built from evidence, analysis and reasoning—can make a field rich with debate and discussion.

Method

Is the methodology used appropriate to the inquiry? Is it sufficient to draw the inferences that they draw? For example, has the author carried out a survey that includes just 3 respondents, as opposed to a survey with 300 respondents? Have they targeted an appropriate demographic or asked appropriate questions? In many cases, an author's methodology might simply be an analysis of existing secondary literature, like most essays. This can be perfectly sufficient, but again you can ask about the quality of that literature review. Using the same questions and methods throughout this chapter, you can ask whether they are using high value, relevant, reliable and timely sources in constructing their analysis. Have they missed important literature or arguments out of the discussion? In effect, we are looking at the quality of the research that has gone into producing the source.

Provenance

Provenance relates to the origin of the source. As such, the source hierarchy above is relevant here. Is the source from a leading and reputable journal or publisher in your discipline or from an unknown online publication? What about the author? Are they a leading professor or academic in your field or a clearly experienced practitioner? Or, are they a student or someone less experienced in the subject? As always, the opinions expressed may still be valid or valuable, but your own arguments will be more persuasive if you link to more authoritative sources.

Timeliness

What is "timely" depends on the context. More recent and up-to-date research is likely to be timely, because the author is likely to be aware of the latest thinking and developments in the field. As such, it will often be better referring to a source from 2020 than from 1950. The ideas, data and theories in your field might have developed considerably in the intervening 70 years!

Nevertheless, historic sources may be equally or even more "timely" if they are closer in time to a specific event under discussion. Certainly, this is the case for primary sources from a historical context, such as a letter written about an event under discussion from 200 years previous. An older source might also be used when citing a particular idea or author from a previous time, such as referring to a famous theory developed in the 1960s. Even so, a recent article providing a modern critical analysis upon that theory might still be an important, if not actually preferable, source to include.

Empirical Research

Most essays at university are based on a literature review of available primary and secondary sources. However, in some disciplines, or further on in your degree, you may have the opportunity or requirement to undertake empirical research.

4. Research

What we really mean by this is carrying out your *own* experiment or study to create your own primary materials from which you can evaluate the findings. We usually separate empirical research into two main methods: *quantitative* (based on generating or compiling quantifiable data) and *qualitative* (based on generating non-numerical information, such as opinions, ideas or feedback).

There is guidance out there on developing suitable methodologies for empirical research and, as this book is focused on essay writing, it is beyond the focus here. What I would say is that if you are given a choice to use empirical research in your essay or dissertation, I would avoid it unless you feel it is absolutely necessary. In some disciplines it may be required or very clearly expected. In others, it might be your choice.

Carrying out reliable and valuable empirical research requires a lot of work, particularly in terms of designing and justifying your choice of research method. It also involves a lot of additional work, such as transcribing interviews, carrying out data analysis or producing tables and graphs. You will often need to obtain ethics approval if your empirical research involves human subjects (e.g., interviewees) or other ethical concerns (e.g., potentially impacting the natural environment). It is really about what research question you really want to ask: if you can ask a slightly different question or can answer it just as effectively by reviewing existing literature, then take that option.

How Many Sources?

This is an extremely common question I get asked by students. Many students have the impression that there is a required minimum number of sources they need to include to get a good grade. Many tutors will say, "It's quality, not quantity." In fact, that is only a half-truth. I am here to tell you the whole truth: the number of sources you have *does* matter. There is no minimum amount. Certainly, you could get an excellent grade with a source for every 250 words (being 8 sources for a 2,000-word essay). But why try and reach the minimum? A 2000-word essay with 16 sources will be far more impressive! Having lots of sources indicates that the student has done lots of rigorous and effective research, that they can incorporate different points and ideas from across the field, and that they have efficiently absorbed and produced useful conclusions. It also makes a paper more persuasive, as it demonstrates that the writer knows the subject and relies on a greater volume of evidence.

However, it is true to say that it is predominantly about *quality*. Thinking about our source hierarchy above, 5 strong academic articles is worth far more than 10 poor quality websites. Commentary and studies by leading academics in your field or on that subtopic will be worth infinitely more than an essay published online by an unrelated company or an unknown author. Sources speaking to the subject matter or supporting the arguments and conclusions being drawn are worth more than sources added to look good but offering little evidential value. So, if deciding whether to add a small number of sources or whether to add more, always go for more. However, we are only ever talking about high quality, effective and appropriate sources!

3. Expert Tips on Becoming an Efficient Researcher

Now we know what you are looking for, this section is loaded with handy tips and guidance on how to become an effective and efficient researcher.

- ✓ **Remember the three steps of research: Foundations, Framing and Focusing**

As discussed in Chapter 1, research is at the heart of the academic essay and forms the lifeblood of academia. Do not be concerned if your research feels like it takes time: it should! That is the very point. Within that, recognize that research can shift from being broad in focus to being narrow in focus and back again. You might start by reading broadly around the essay topic, looking for connections, debates, relevant ideas, or areas of ambiguity and uncertainty. At this stage you are reading expansively and with an open mind. Notetaking might not be as central in this foundational stage: it is more about reading a lot and familiarizing yourself with the area.

If the subject area is immediately appreciable or, after engaging in foundational reading, you begin to get more familiar, you start the process of framing the different debates, views and ideas. From here, you can formulate your own ideas and start shaping your argument, while also mapping out your essay plan (see the next chapter). You will also start more rigorous notetaking, as you will have a much better idea of what is noteworthy and what is not. Eventually, once you know your core arguments and have begun compiling key resources, your research will naturally narrow in on the specific evidence, materials or ideas you need to execute your paper.

✓ **Start with the easy stuff**
Where should you begin? Well, as noted in Chapter 2, I would first go back to everything that you have covered on the essay topic in your course, be it lecture notes, handouts, assigned reading, and so on. Also, go to the textbooks. Textbooks are usually written with the student in mind and their focus is usually to explain, simplify, break down or synthesize understanding on a particular subject matter. If it is available, start with the easy stuff that defines the topic in an understandable manner and begins to introduce key questions, terms, debates or issues in a manageable format. Chapters in many edited volumes, such as research handbooks, can also be effective at doing this, largely by compiling existing knowledge on a particular subject. What is more, textbooks and research handbooks will usually link you to important articles and sources on that subject matter. (TIP: Search in your institution's library for terms like "research handbook" or just "handbook" around certain subjects, as these are common titles for edited volumes.)

✓ **Continually try to narrow your research focus and aims**

It is completely normal to start researching and to suddenly become overwhelmed with the different sources of information available. That is the very nature of research. There will be times where you will feel you are losing track of where you are going, just as there will be times when you know exactly what you are looking for. Simply see your research aims and focus as organic and know that they will move with your research process. In other words, keep an open mind to your research aims adjusting to the research you are finding and frequently stop to break down or summarize your key research focal points. Try as much as possible, within this process, to keep your research question and aims as narrow and clear as possible.

✓ **Accept that there are lots of rabbit holes and red herrings**

By this I mean that you will sometimes spend time reading or digesting things that do not end up being useful to your essay. This is not to say that they are *useless*. You will be learning and developing your broader knowledge and expertise all the time, while becoming familiar with the broader literature field. What is more, you need to know what you *do not* need to read, to know what you *do* need to read! Do not feel worried or frustrated if a particular direction you go in your research comes to a dead end. That is just the nature of crafting an interesting essay where the ideas are largely formulated by absorbing the wider materials.

✓ **Do not be afraid to skim-read and be ruthless in locating relevant points**

A big part of research is continually refining your focus and awareness of the literature, such that you become more discerning in knowing what is relevant to you and what is not. Be as ruthless as you need to be in locating relevant sources and sections within sources. Just read the abstracts and keywords of sources and articles initially, to see if they are *likely* to be relevant. If an article's abstract suggests the source is making one broad point, but not adding much more to your discussion beyond that, just copy-and-paste the abstract into your notes and don't bother reading the whole thing. If an article explains the literature field and aims in the introduction, but then moves into a detailed analysis of data or of case studies with little further contribution in the main body, then skip to the conclusion.

If a source is simply far too complex and you are not even sure if you are taking anything from it, make a note of it and move on. If a source sounds like it *might* be relevant, but you are not sure, do a rapid skim-read or search for key terms in the document and discern whether there are parts within in it that are relevant. If there is, maybe skip to those parts or read across them if the context will assist or offer more.

In other words, just be ruthless in trying to find relevant, useful or interesting information that might contribute to your essay's argument or discussion. Some sources will be rich with lots of great information and links to other sources; some might only contain one valuable sentence. You are treasure hunting remember!

✓ **Use sources to find sources!**
A huge aspect of research is linking between sources. I find half of my research sources by going to the sources cited by someone else. If there is a detailed and well-referenced piece of work on the subject, use it not only to understand the field further and to take in viewpoints and hypotheses for your essay, but to also link off to all those other sources and materials. Research is sometimes like building a web, where you follow links between sources, ideas and materials.

✓ **Develop an efficient notetaking method**
The beauty of research is that no one person has the same technique or method as another. You will have methods that particularly suit you or which you find

quicker or easier than others. Continually reflect on your notetaking processes and look for changes that will make it more efficient, more effective, or both.

I personally open a new Word document and put 'Research Notes' as the title. I then add sources with their title or URL underlined. Underneath each source I will write sections or paragraphs of notes that I take from that source. I also add a subheading to each section of discussion, in bold, so that I can later read through the whole document and easily get a snapshot of what each section or paragraph discusses. Underneath each of these shorthand subheadings I either copy-and-paste a segment of the document or summarize parts of it in my own words. I usually include the page number as well. Just for example (turn overleaf):

Example of my own personal note-taking system
Matthewson (2013) – The Practical Issues of Notetaking
Everyone has different styles / Common methods
3. Every individual has their own style and method of notetaking, with each developing their own efficiencies or idiosyncrasies. In fact, there are several different methods of notetaking, including Cornell Method, Outlining Method and the Mapping Method.
Useful research study on notetaking efficiency
4. – Points to Marr (2010) – An Efficiency Analysis of Notetaking Styles, that interestingly tested different notetaking methods and argues that they are all capable of being equally efficient and speedy, depending on the neurological characteristics of the notetaker.
Most important things are speed, distraction and navigability
6. Everyone has their own styles, but the most important thing is about the notetaker's own ability to produce notes quickly with minimal distraction

> from their observations. It is also essential that the notetaker can quickly navigate and understand their notes after a long break from them.
>
> Stark (2015) – Technological Solutions to Notetaking Inefficiencies
> And so on...

Because I summarize everything with a short and concise subheading, it forces me to understand and succinctly explain what has been said. Even if I copy-and-paste a passage or quote from someone else, instead of having to re-read it later out of context, I can get a clue or summary of what the quote or passage is saying from my subheadings. Curiously, any notes made in my own words under the subheading I will indent with a hyphen (see example in the middle of my notes above, before the word *Points*), whereas I dispense with the hyphen for directly copied passages.

This all sounds confusing. Do not worry, this is just *my* research method, which works for me. I cannot really explain it! The result in preparing for an essay is that I might have a 50-page document of notes, all with subheadings explaining what the notes are about. (For my PhD, I had multiple documents for different subtopics, with some being 300 pages in length!) Protect your research notes documents doggedly. Email them to yourself at the end of the day, as well as backing them up in two places. They will be gold dust when it comes to producing your essays.

✓ **Use your institution's library, Google Scholar and relevant databases**
Most universities and colleges have a fantastic digital library, with subscriptions to a huge wealth of databases and repositories. Become familiar with the techniques and tools to find resources across your institution's library, including undertaking any training or guidance to support you. These types of sources are likely to be 'higher quality' than what you would find by just relying on Google.

That said, I strongly recommend you also use Google Scholar (scholar.google.com). While their search algorithm is always improving, it provides a massive database of links to most quality academic materials. Note that many of the articles linked on Google Scholar or in other databases might require you to sign in 'Via your Institution', where you will use your student login credentials to gain access. Finally, make considerable use of any discipline-specific databases or repositories you are signposted to. Your tutors will want you to use these; they probably use them too!

✓ **Use Boolean operators and truncation**

Boolean operators are simple and essential tools in database research and online research. Several key Boolean operators include AND, OR, NOT, quotation marks (" "), parentheses (( )), asterisks (*) and *intitle*. The addition of these into your search phrases can really help you narrow down or draw more accurate search results. You can also use what is known as "truncation" to target a broader list of potential words.

Here is a helpful summary of these operators:
- **Quotation Marks:** Placing words between quotation marks means that the search engine will search for words *in that exact order*. You may not realize it, but unless instructed a search engine will automatically search for all words in any order. It may prioritize the words first in the list or look for similar patterns, but this is not likely to be effective. Say you were looking for an exact phrase, such as *transnational law of the sea*. If I typed into Google just those words, it would search for anything containing *sea* AND *law* AND *and* AND *of* AND *transnational*. This yields 36.3 million results. If I type in "transnational law of the sea", within quotation marks, it looks for that *exact* order of words. This yields only 5 results on Google, all of which link to my article with that title.

4. Research

- **AND:** Most search engines will assume an AND between your search terms unless instructed otherwise. It ultimately means that the results should include both words on either side of the word. For example, if searching 'dog AND cat', it will produce search results where both dog *and* cat are mentioned. Note: Depending on the search algorithm, it will not just list results randomly, but will try to place results in order of relevance. For example, it will place results with the search words in the title, subtitle, opening lines or metadata much higher than results where the words are only briefly mentioned at the end.

- **OR:** You can probably guess that OR is an instruction to search for *either* word. It is, in effect, telling the search engine to merge two sets of results into one: one including the first word and another including the other word. As before, it will prioritize results with greater relevance or stronger mentions of either word. So, if we now search for 'dog OR cat', we will get a much larger list of results because it will give us any article containing *either* word, instead of both. It can be useful in combination with AND, so that you could search something like 'dog AND cat OR kitten'.

- **NOT:** This is a helpful operator for excluding certain words from search results. It is extremely helpful when certain phrases or popular combinations are contaminating your results. For example, say you are looking for information on the architecture of Sheffield Wednesday FC's football stadium, Hillsborough Stadium. However, as you read through results you are constantly getting papers that are more focused on the Hillsborough disaster in 1989, rather than on the design of the stadium itself. A useful addition might be to add 'NOT disaster NOT tragedy' to the search, which will remove all results containing the words disaster or tragedy. Just for example, a search might be: *"Hillsborough Stadium"* architecture OR design NOT disaster NOT tragedy. A common symbol used instead of NOT is a hyphen (-) just before the word and this is what I mostly use. So, your search could actually be: *"Hillsborough Stadium" architecture OR design -disaster -tragedy.*

- **Parentheses:** Much like in arithmetic, search engines will often complete searches on terms inside parentheses (( )) before looking at the rest of the search term. It therefore helps to group certain words or phrases together. For example, you would yield very different results between the following two searches: *(dog OR cat) AND children* versus *dog OR (cat AND children).* The first term is more narrow (prioritizing articles specifically with dog or cat mentioned, plus children); the second is broader (prioritizing results with *either* cat and children mentioned, or simply, dog).

It is worth noting, however, that not all search engines use all Boolean operators in the same way, and you may need to check the specific operators (usually adapted from these classics) in each search engine. For example, Google Search does not recognize parentheses, although many other search engines do.

- **Truncation:** Truncation is not so much an operator, as a common search trick, which is extremely useful. It is simply the idea of searching for shorter "root" word stems that can have additional letters or suffixes added, whenever you are interested in all those wider words. For example, say you are searching for anything relating to *employee, employer, employment, employing,* many search engines will include all of these in the results if you just search for "employ". Another example might be searching "build" if you are looking for words like *build, builder, building, builder* and so on.

- **Asterisk:** The asterisk (*) is a wildcard operator that can have different meanings on different engines. Its most common meaning is as a truncation device. We mentioned before that searching for "employ" or "build" might generate results with longer words stemming from those root words. However, some search engines will only search for "employ" or "build", without extending the word. They will instead expect you to add an asterisk to widen the word stem, e.g., employ* or build*.

  In many search engines, the asterisk can also be used to create a blank space for *any* word to appear in the middle of a phrase. For example, say you want to search for results that prioritize where a dog does something to a cat. It could be chasing a cat, or hugging a cat, or licking a cat, and so on. Then you could search "dog * a cat" and the search engine would locate results with phrases saying exactly this with any other combination of words in the middle.

- **Intitle:** The *intitle:* operator narrows results to those where the word or phrase appears in the title. It is very useful for reordering the search results to give greater priority to certain search terms or for when you only want articles specifically on a subject. For example, when searching on Google, I get 29 million results for *"dogs and cats"*, because it is searching for anything with that phrase *anywhere* inside each result. I only get 407,000 results for *intitle:"cats and dogs"*, which is purely searching for results with that phrase in the title.

✓ **Mix up the medium**

There are lots of advantages to using digital resources, not least the ability to search within documents and to copy passages. However, it is also good for your concentration and focus if you can vary it up sometimes too and reduce screen time. Is there a physical book available or can you access a resource on your

Kindle? Maybe do this occasionally instead and enjoy reading and researching in a different format and in a different setting.

✓ **Do not worry about referencing until later**

It is important you make a note of the title of any source and the author, so that you can later find it again via Google Scholar or another database. However, do not worry about writing everything needed to reference it or about putting it into the correct citation method, unless you are certain it is going to be used. You can do all that in one go at the end of your essay, when you go through and put all your references into the proper format. You may also be using a referencing software (see below), which would automatically do all of this for you. However, as noted, still do make sure you make a note of the title, author and year. It is very frustrating when you forget to do this and cannot later find the same source again.

✓ **Save useful passages and quotes that can be reused; but also paraphrase ideas where you can**

Sometimes in your essay it is good to include direct quotes. Especially if the quote is eloquent on a particular point or does a great job of emphasizing the point being made. In most cases, however, you are better served by paraphrasing the ideas of others in your work (see more in Chapter 9). When making notes, do consider the types of quotes and passages that might be suitable for including as a direct quote. Perhaps quotes that express a point very poignantly or with great emphasis. Otherwise, try to either write a summary of anything you have read in your own words or, at the very least, copy it and then add a summary or subheading in your own words succinctly summarizing what it says. Not only will this help you to understand it better when you come back to it later, out of context, but it will also help you to memorize and absorb the things you are reading. What is more, it gives you great practice at writing concisely (see more in Chapter 9) and forces you to check your own understanding of the things you are reading.

✓ **Look for more recent sources and then work back in time**
As noted, a big part of the research process is finding sources linked from other sources. You also want to use sources that are up-to-date or timely. It can be good to ensure that you find plenty of sources that are particularly recent. These are likely to contain an updated perspective on academic contributions to that discussion, as well as any noteworthy recent additions into the field of inquiry. What is more, it can enable you to link back to a greater number of sources by linking back in a reverse-chronology. A useful feature on Google Scholar, for example, is looking at 'Cited By', which will look forward in time at later articles that cite the current source under focus. Alternatively, include a search limitation on how recent the sources should be, e.g., selecting 'No older than 2018'.

✓ **Do a Google search and include the term "PDF"**
Depending on your discipline, I find this to be a really effective mechanism for locating more official publications and resources than a standard Google search would produce. For example, it might lead to official reports or widely circulated studies on a particular topic, as well as documents produced by an official body or institution.

✓ **Try different and more specific search terms**
Instead of just searching for your subject matter, once you have an idea what your essay is focusing on, try being more specific. Say I was writing a paper on the difficulties with achieving a circular economy, just as an example. Then I might search for the terms "circular economy" and "weaknesses". But then also think of synonyms or alternative ways of saying something. I could then go for "circular economy" with "drawbacks", "failure", "feasibility", "problems", and so on. Try different searches and experiment. It is a treasure hunt after all!

✓ **Use references to whole books on Amazon to make certain well-known assertions**

By this, I mean that you could take a widely accepted idea or promoted view and simply search for a book listed on Amazon that is dedicated to that topic. You could read the abstract on the book or the first few pages, to check the book is suitable and relevant. If it is, just drop in a reference to the *whole* book. Say I was making a point about growing concerns about corporate greenwashing, I might do an Amazon search for "greenwashing" and, *voila*, I could cite Frances Bowen's book, *After Greenwashing: Symbolic Corporate Environmentalism and Society*. Amazon book search is also particularly helpful for its "Look Inside" feature, which often allows you to peruse the table of contents and first few pages of most books in the world!

✓ **Have imaginary conversations with the authors about their work**

This relates back to the 'Thinking Critically' discussion in Chapter 3. The point is not just to read everything as truth, but to be prepared to question the ideas, assertions, analyses and arguments of others as you are reading them. You are developing yourself as an authority in your specific subtopic, so do not be afraid to question the veracity or accuracy of ideas propounded by others or, indeed, to fully agree with them and find them persuasive. The more you read in your subject area, the more you will have an opinion and will enjoy expressing that opinion in your interactions with the literature field. Do not be afraid to even speak out loud to the people you are reading!

✓ **Continually take stock**

When does the research process end? Only you can know. The reality is that research can keep going forever, with the research's focus becoming more nuanced and aimed at multiple different directions. It is truly never-ending. As above, you need to continually be refining and narrowing your research aims and be ruthless with seeking out the materials you specifically need to construct your essay.

A good way to continually take stock is to occasionally move from making research notes over to mapping out and planning your essay (see the next chapter). In this process, you can more clearly and succinctly spell out the core arguments and focus of your essay, as well as examine what literature you have on the different components that need to be covered and what literature or evidence might still be needed. You may know of certain parts where you do not currently have the notes, but you have a good idea of where you will quickly find them when it comes to writing up. You may realize that you need to tweak the focus and direction of your essay to better cater to the direction that your research has taken you. In the end, if you have a good looking essay plan, which is likely to contain arguments that are persuasive and rigorous, and making use of a reasonable amount of evidence, then you will have done all the research you need to do.

5. Planning

1. Always Be Planning

Planning is not just something you do before you begin writing. It is a continuous process that should start as soon as you receive your assessment instructions, right up until you save your final submission. It is also a fluid and dynamic process. Your planning should be responsive to the discoveries and directions that your research takes you, as well as to the entire process of writing up and shaping your essay. Planning can at one point be looking at the wider scale, shaping your entire essay's focus; at other times, it might be zoning in on a sequence of sentences or point of analysis inside the essay.

One of the most important and defining steps of essay writing is the planning process, where you map out your essay's *outline*. In many senses, writing the essay is easy once you know what you are going to say. While your research is happening, you should continuously map out the skeleton of your essay. The writing part is then simply a task of adding the flesh to the bones. If you have made a good plan and done relevant research, the writing part will be far quicker, easier and more enjoyable. Therefore, *create a specific document where you are continuously drawing out the map of your essay*, with the key sections and points under them. Start it as soon as you can because it is an organic document that you can keep playing around with and trying different combinations.

Effective essay planning makes the entire academic process so much more enjoyable. It also makes essays far less intimidating. At first, you might be panicked to have to write 2,000 words on a topic in a way that is worthy of an outstanding mark. But, when you consider that your Introduction and Conclusion might be 10% of the words each, that only leaves around 1,600 words. If there are around 200 words in a paragraph and you map out what each paragraph will discuss, then you only have to discuss around 8 different points for the whole essay. Seen in that way, it is actually a much simpler task. What is more, effective planning will also give your essay excellent structure and coherence.

It is worth pointing out that we are talking here about mapping out a standard university or academic essay. Therefore, this chapter does not discuss the specific outlining models you might use in more specific assignments. For example, for a reflective essay, you might be expected to adopt a Gibbs or Kolb cycle of reflection as a structural guide. For a law problem question, students will commonly adopt an IRAC structure (Issue-Rule-Application-Conclusion). Similarly, if producing a scientific paper in a scientific discipline, you may be required to adopt a scientific paper structure with Materials and Methods, Results and Discussion sections. We are discussing standard essay plans that do not have such prescribed structural formats. Even so, the broader issues of time management, planning and argument sequencing in this chapter still apply to all such forms of essay.

Time to Get Planning

As highlighted in Chapter 2, the sooner you start thinking about your essay plan, the sooner your subconsciousness can beaver away at refining, reformulating and perfecting it. It is not just the planning you do in your head that is important: it is also about frequently referring to a document that has your essay outline mapped out, where you can try different formulations and sequences of discussion. Planning is equally about refining your overall research question and aims. As highlighted in Chapter 4, research is an organic process and your precise arguments or research aims will probably adapt as the research process takes place. Your plan is therefore a living document that you interact with from start to finish. Similarly, if you recall the 9 Fs of Essay Process in Chapter 1 (Foundations → Framing → Focusing → Forming → Finding → Fixing →

5. Planning

Formatting → Final Submission → Feedback), it is clear that planning plays a part in every stage in the process.

So, as soon as you can, start your mind thinking about our essay plan. It can help to get a draft document or pen to paper as early as possible, to start playing around with ideas, concepts and known areas to cover. The sooner you start reducing your knowledge to paper and trying to succinctly summarize the key issues and areas you want to cover, the sooner your essay map and plan will begin to emerge. Importantly, this will significantly the quality and efficiency of your research process, by helping you focus sooner on the sources you need finalize construction of your plan. Given that planning is an essential practice that permeates the entire essay process, it is vitally important to adopt effective time management techniques and tips:

✓ **Plan by starting with your deadline and working backwards**

The first and most important step is to generate a plan that acknowledges the various stages—or F's—involved in completing the essay. If you start by looking at the date of your final deadline on a calendar, then "work backwards" by estimating how many days are needed for each of the stages. How many days something takes will depend a lot on your work or life commitments, and ability to focus solely on the essay, as well as your areas of strength and weakness. In general, though, you are far better assuming the worst and hoping for the best. For example, if you think formatting might take 1 or 2 days, then allow for 2 days. These things are almost always tighter than we expect and we always hit unforeseen delays. Using the 9 Fs for inspiration, the key 7 stages you might want to include in your calculations are:

(1) Final Deadline →
(2) Proofreading/Editing →
(3) Referencing/Formatting →
(4) Write Up →

(5) Focused Research →
(6) Essay Outline →
(7) Broader Research →

If you prefer, you can see further guidance on this in the Essay Timeline Template, downloadable for free at www.academyworks.co.

✓ **Draw a timeline setting out key "milestones" with their deadlines**
Using these projected timescales, draw up a timeline that sets out the dates by which the various stages will be completed. It always amazes students, when they do this, just how little time they have. One of the first things I do with a dissertation student is help them work out a timeline. Often they are shocked to discover that they should have started work on their essay yesterday!

✓ **Work against the deadlines**
You can use the deadlines to measure progress. It is also a useful way of preventing procrastination and ensuring that you keep on track. It is there to help you, but do not let it cause you panic or stress. We all have periods of higher productivity and periods of lower productivity. The key is ensuring that you maximize on those periods of better productivity and try to minimize the length and disruption of lower productivity periods. Your performance against the milestone deadlines may go up or down, so try not to panic. However, do use it to prevent yourself from falling too far behind. Being able to work against your own self-imposed deadlines, with the use of self-discipline and time management, is a crucial life skill.

✓ **Set reminders on your calendar for key milestones**
I have had too many students email at the last minute to say that they lost track of the date, or they got dates mixed up, so were not aware that the deadline was so close. I empathize because, being a human myself, I have made the same

mistake with other deadlines in my life. The only way I deal with it now is using a calendar app to input key dates, with reminder notifications to come in days or weeks before deadlines. It sounds fiddly, but it is super important not to miss deadlines and to keep yourself alert to the little milestones, commitments and tasks you are managing.

✓ **Do not be afraid to move between stages if it helps**

The stages of essay production are relatively linear: you cannot format something before you have written it, for example! Nevertheless, do not feel rigidly trapped to the stages. During periods of lower productivity, or when I am particularly tired, I usually switch to less intensive tasks such as going through my research notes and copying notes and comments across into the sections of my essay, ready to be fleshed out later. Alternatively, I might proofread the writing I have already done.

✓ **Perform occasional knowledge audits and plan reviews**

Information gathering is something that occurs through much of the essay production process: in the foundational stages, you are gathering information on the topic to broaden your understanding; whereas, even right up to the formatting stages, you are correcting references and inputting missing links and data sources. Throughout the process, therefore, you should be alert to the knowledge and information you *have*, as compared with the knowledge and information you *need*. As the essay is being formed, you can start to be more precise in terms of the *exact* kinds of sources or information you need. Keeping an eye on this will help you understand your progress against the timelines and whether you need to move between writing or data gathering.

✓ **Act against procrastination**

We all do it. We all get carried away with unessential tasks, when we should be focusing on the pressing ones. We all look at our phones, emails or social media, when we should be working. We all make excuses about why it is good for us to take an extra-long lunch and do something more fun with the afternoon. Sometimes those things *can* be good. As highlighted in Chapter 4, working in regular breaks and rewards is an important aspect of being a successful academic. Nevertheless, those things should never be a replacement for long-term focus and productivity. The most successful students are those who successfully control or resist temptations and distractions. Put in place measures to help you, like putting blockers on distracting social media, putting your phone on silent, or imposing time periods for certain activities. Doing this, and telling yourself it is time to work, is surprisingly empowering!

✓ **Read this whole book**

This entire book informs you on every aspect of the process if you want to produce outstanding essays. While it may seem like some initial time spent up-front by reading it all, it will increase your effectiveness, efficiency and productivity across every area of the essay writing process. The overall time saved and the improvement in grades will more than make up for the small amount of time it takes to read it.

2. Argument Sequencing

A critically important aspect of powerful essay structure is your argument sequencing. I often explain that an essay will be poor if it moves haphazardly from B to E to D to A to C. Take a lot of time to think what your conclusion and overall argument, E, is. From here, work out what would be the logical components to go in B, C and D to reach your final argument in a persuasive and coherent narrative. Then use your introduction, A, to set out the essay's focus and journey to the reader. Therefore, deciding what B, C and D are in your argument sequence is crucial. Think of a coherent and logical series of 'steps', each replete with their own analytical focus, to reach that end goal. In effect, the development of your argument wants to be a gradual progression through steps that need to be addressed, rather than a jumble of ideas.

There is no one single way to write an essay. That said, in most cases, you are likely to want 3 to 4 sections within your essay in addition to the Introduction and Conclusion. For shorter essays, even 2 or 3 "stages" in the main body could suffice. They want to be sufficiently large such that they carry meaning and value as a step in your argument sequencing. In longer essays, you might have 3 or even 4 sections. For a dissertation or larger thesis, it could be 4 to 8 sections (or "chapters"). Looking at the argument sequencing from A to E then, your essay might look something like this.

STEP	CONTENT
A	1. Introduction
B	2. Section
C	3. Section
D	4. Section
E	5. Conclusion

For another example, consider a short essay with 6 paragraphs in total. The sequence of steps from A to F might look this:

STEP	CONTENT
A	Introduction Paragraph
B	Paragraph
C	Paragraph
D	Paragraph

E	Paragraph
F	Concluding Paragraph

The development of your argument sequencing involves thinking about what to analyze in each of these stages in the journey, to lead the reader logically to the conclusion.

Note: I have used the letters A-B-C-D-E just to illustrate the sequential nature of the essay's narrative. If you have sections with headings, you should usually adopt a number ordering system instead of letters.

Sequence Design

Enjoy the process of occasionally stepping away from research to play around with your essay outline. Try different combinations, different section headings, different placement of ideas. It is all about finding a suitable optimum pathway, with a clear and coherent narrative, that takes you to a persuasive argument at E. Fingers crossed, you might even have a *Eureka!* moment, where it all slots nicely into place. I was switching up the sequence for my PhD for three and a half years, but when it finally slotted together it made so much sense and worked perfectly!

As already highlighted, you need to move on from just discussing pros and cons. Remember, you are seeking to persuade the reader of your research findings, so the focus of the essay must be on a sequence of analysis that ultimately leads to that conclusion. As such, try to move on from thinking "Advantages" in the first section, "Disadvantages" in the next, followed by "Which is better?" in the third. You can develop your argument sequence far more creatively. Perhaps you can critique different theories in each section, or deal with matters chronologically, or address different potential solutions to a problem, or focus on different case studies. Think smartly as well. You are likely to design earlier steps with some "description" in mind (see Chapter 3), giving you a chance to concisely introduce and define key issues and concepts to the reader, while also progressing your analysis and argument sequence.

One way to help decide on the different stages in the essay's sequence is to begin combining your notes or ideas together into different categories or groupings. Look for common themes or ways to associate your notes into discrete categories. One way of doing this could be using a brainstorm that compiles all your thoughts and notes into a diagram with everything interconnected. Alternatively, imagine you are filing everything away in a database and it all needs to be categorized for later reference. Once you have assorted your ideas into discrete topics like this, you can more easily see the potential stages that might need to be arranged into an order. You might also determine that some concepts or notes do not fit neatly into the existing groupings and might not, therefore, be suitable for inclusion.

The most important thing is to focus on achieving your argument and thinking about the steps needed to reach that goal. Earlier in the essay, the stages are likely to be setting out the problems and introducing the core hypothesis of your essay. Later stages are likely to be addressing specific issues raised by the hypothesis or dealing with potential counterarguments. Similarly, the early stages in an essay are likely to be on the less controversial matters, such as introducing existing theories or established concepts, before moving into the more "contentious" issues raised by the essay's argument. You might also ask, "What does the reader need to know—and when?" In the earlier stages, you might therefore be explaining the nature of the issue or field of inquiry, after which you justify the essay's position and rationale, before finally addressing questions and challenges that the reader might have in mind.

Likely in the Early Stages	Likely in the Later Stages
• Explaining issue or existing ideas in the field of inquiry • Rationalising your argument or position • Dealing with the least contentious points	• Addressing counterarguments or potential problems with argument • Resolving questions or concerns that the reader might have • Dealing with more complex issues

3. Producing Your Essay Outline

Here are some more important tips on producing your essay skeleton.

✓ Focus on the argument

This was stressed in Chapter 3 but bears loud repeating. Do not spend long parts of your essay discussing things that are interesting, just because they are interesting. The focus of everything is your core hypothesis, position or argument: the essay plan should be dedicated to this. Everything should be serving to clarify this position or to advance it. If in the process of developing your ideas you come up with some interesting yet unrelated findings, then great! These are fertile territory for future research, dissertation topics or papers you might want to later write and even publish. But do not use up words on them just because they are cool or interesting, unless they advance the position or objectives of the paper.

✓ Use section headings in your plan, even if not in the final essay

For smaller essays of up to 1,500 words, you may even be able to dispense with having sections with headings in the essay. Anything above this and you are likely to achieve better structure and clarity of the "journey" for your reader if you neatly compartmentalize issues into sections with headings. However, even if your final essay does not have titled sections, it is important to still map out your essay skeleton with imaginary sections in mind. This will improve the structure and flow of your final essay, as well as help the reader to identify the steps in the journey. It will also help you as you map your ideas out.

✓ **Use bullet points**

A skeleton of your essay needs to be just that. Try not to just compile loads of notes under each section heading within the essay outline. You can certainly do this in a separate document or somewhere separate to your skeleton outline, but make sure you keep somewhere a concise overall map of the essay. Under each section, use bullet points or concise notes to summarize the different points or issues that will be covered under that section. Being able to concisely summarize the issues to be covered is a good way to check that the overall plan is coherent and that each section is well-balanced in terms of length and detail.

✓ **Keep in mind the likely available word counts**

It is amazing how quickly the available word count starts evaporating once you start compiling all the things that need to be covered. Keep in mind the realistic space available for each component. If you bear in mind that the Introduction and Conclusion each use around 10% of the word count and that paragraphs could be around 200-250 words, give or take, then you can estimate the likely available word space for each component.

✓ **Aim for balance and symmetry**

It is not always the case that concepts or issues will be neatly equal in terms of the space needed to cover them. However, in designing your essay, try to find balance and harmony where you can. If one section is 300 words, but another is 1,000 words, you might want to reconsider your categorization of the issues or refine the focus and aims of each section. Alternatively, you might break them up differently or merge certain parts together, so that the sections are closer in size.

- ✓ **Refer back to the assessment instructions and marking criteria occasionally**

Remember that your essay needs to also hit the brief, as discussed in Chapter 2. Avoid working hard on an essay plan, only to later see the assessment guidance and realize you are not, for example, "discussing" an idea, or "comparing" competing ideas, or are missing key substantive topics in focus. It is therefore important to occasionally switch back to the assessment brief while planning to ensure that you are hitting the points that need to be covered.

- ✓ **If you write a lot, you might use fewer bullet points in the plan; if you struggle to write, you might use more**

It is about making your skeleton plan work for you, so lay out the components in way that makes sense to you. You might find that if you struggle to generate ideas while writing or do not feel confident on all the detail, then it is helpful to add more bullet points in your plan.

- ✓ **If you are struggling, take a break from it for a few days and come back to it**

Your plan is a living document that should be worked on early in the process and continue to be shaped as you progress through your research and writing. Do not panic if it does not fall into shape the first day you look at it. If you start planning early and leave sufficient time, you could step away from it for a couple of days and come back to it with fresh eyes. Or, even better, use this time to continue reading around the subject to get further inspiration and see different approaches to it.

- ✓ **If you are really struggling, you can even try freewriting**

This is a widely used practice among even the most experienced writers. We can all suffer from "writer's block" or "blank page syndrome". First up, if you are still struggling to write, it is often because you need to read more around your subject and continue making notes and building your critical insights. But, if you have done a huge quantity of research and are still feeling like you lack a clear path through, then definitely start freewriting. This means just writing whatever comes into your mind and keeping going. Start discussing concepts, explaining points, introducing arguments, carrying out critical analyses. Do not worry if it is rubbish or wrong. The very point with freewriting is to write freely without any such concerns, expecting that you will likely delete everything at the end of it. It is just a process to get into that writing mindset and can allow ideas to emerge by letting your writing flow.

✓ **Play around with your essay's title**
If you have the opportunity or freedom to set your own essay title, do it. Look at peer-reviewed journal articles for ideas and clues about how an academic paper might be titled. Having a title is great for making your paper feel like a standalone piece of work that is dedicated to its focus and hypotheses, rather than an "assignment" for your tutor. It also significantly improves structure by signalling to the reader the topic and general direction of the paper. If you can set your own title, then the ongoing essay planning process is also an opportunity to experiment with different essay titles, depending on how the paper shapes up. The title wants to be super concise and punchy, effectively indicating the subject and direction of the paper.

✓ **Share your essay plan with your supervisor or tutor, if available**
For larger pieces of work, like a dissertation, you will have a supervisor. Your essay map is a crucially important thing that your supervisor or tutor can really help you with. Discussing it in detail with them could give you useful ideas to refine the plan and structure, as well as ensuring you are covering the detail or analysis needed in the right places. It also forces you to check that your essay plan is coherent and that you, yourself, can speak to it. Do not do this at the last minute. It's amazing how quickly a deadline that is months away can come

around. I have had too many students who left it to the last second to finally send me a plan, only to discover there was some work needed on the overall direction, focus and layout of their arguments.

- ✓ **Start a second essay map, where you begin to copy your research notes and ideas**

You have now got your essay outline which you can keep playing around with. It's time to make a *copy* of your essay outline to "fill out" and to begin copying across all the notes, references and findings from your research notes into the relevant sections. At first the document will be long, messy and unwieldy. But, when ready, you can work through *condensing* those notes into your own writing, with all the materials and references immediately to hand within the section. Each section will start getting shorter, as it converts from a mass of notes into your own writing with those notes just being referenced in the text. Important note: Instead of 'cutting' all your notes from your research document into your essay plan, use copy-and-paste. It's useful to keep a duplicate of *all* your notes together in your research notes document, in case they get edited over or lost and you need to come back to them.

- ✓ **Do not be afraid to start writing and populating sections or components**

More will be discussed on transitioning into writing below. If you suddenly have a thought about how you might explain or discuss something, write it. There is no better way to improve your writing than to just get it down and then later refine and improve it. Just draft ideas, arguments, concepts or explanations as they come to you. You may or may not use what you write, or you might later refine it, but it's all part of building your essay and your accompanying notes and materials.

4. Get Ready to Write

You can begin jotting down ideas or drafting components at any stage. However, you may want to have a clear essay plan in place and a suitable collection of notes and evidence to use, before you steam ahead with writing. As discussed, writing is so much easier, efficient and enjoyable once you have a clear outline in place, with most of the materials and notes you are going to use added into the map. That said, you Do not need to spend forever planning and compiling research, without ever getting round to writing. Those tasks are continuous and you can always dip back into them, even after you have begun writing.

Most importantly, the writing process is not a one-stop affair. An excellent essay is usually the product of multiple refinements and several proofreads, edits and amendments. Most of us write by getting everything down, even if it's too big or is a little "rough around the edges", and we then work back through it to fix errors, make it more concise and refined, and ensure it has a nice flow. As soon as you have a general map in place and a good idea of the types of materials and evidence you will use, or where you will find them, then it's time to get that first draft down.

While it might be easier for you to produce your initial draft in sequential order, working through the sections and components as they arise in the essay, there is nothing to say you must do it that way. You might prefer to draft the first section and third section, before then doing the introduction and second section. It's fine if you want to do this. Just write things in the order that works for you. Again, having a reasonable idea of what will go where, makes this decision easier. Getting writing will help you to also formulate and enhance your ideas, as well as help you identify gaps in your knowledge or research. You will also get a better sense of the space needed to cover different components or how different components fit or Do not fit neatly into your essay map. Remember, you must always go back and work to refine your writing, so Do not worry if it does not quite come out right the first time you write it. The most important thing is the quality of your subsequent proofreading, editing and improving of your first draft.

Now we are halfway through this book, you might be wondering how you are going to remember everything that is being covered. I do recognize that this book contains a lot of detailed information and explanations. You have probably already lost track of a few things. However, please do not worry. I have also produced a helpful checklist booklet to support you. The checklist booklet lists all the key tips and steps that need to be considered at every stage throughout the entire process, acting as an aide-mémoire to everything in this book. A warning therefore: the booklet will not make be any use at all unless you have read this book first! The checklist booklet can be downloaded for free at www.academyworks.co. But, like I say, do not think that the booklet will cover the rest of the book sufficiently. Far from it! But it is there for when you have finished the book and come to your next assignment. With that in mind, let us now explain all the important secrets of essay structure.

6. Structure

1. The Fish Skeleton

You might be aware of just how important essay structuring is. There is a reason why thousands of students are asking Google questions like, "How do I structure an essay?" or "What goes in an essay introduction?" It is also one of the most common points of feedback raised by tutors. It's so important because all the other core criteria that we want to see in your essays—such as knowledge, understanding, communication, use of materials, analysis, and so on—hinge heavily on being presented in a clear, coherent and methodical manner. You could have all the ideas and excellent materials to refer to, but without good structuring it will be a poor essay.

Most of the guidance you find when Googling about this just stresses the need for an introduction and conclusion. For sure, these are important components, such that they have a whole chapter dedicated to them (the next chapter). However, powerful and effective structure is something much bigger, permeating throughout your entire essay. Essay structure is, quite simply, all about ensuring that your reader can naturally follow the "journey" through your paper. The reader wants to always have a sense of where they are in the journey and where they are going. Without this, your reader will become lost and confused. Poor structure, therefore, is where ideas and points arise at random junctures with a lack of coherence or linking between topics, meaning that key points are not expressed clearly or effectively. This will only frustrate your marker and will make your arguments and demonstration of knowledge much weaker.

I am an exponent of the fish skeleton analogy for essay structure. Look at the fish skeleton in this picture as an outline map of an essay:

How to Write Amazing Essays

The 'Fish Skeleton' Essay Outline
Image Credit: Author's Own

The head is your *introduction* that tells the reader, in effect, "This is where we are, and this is where we are going." It introduces key themes and situates the reader in the "problem", as well as spelling out the direction and focus of the essay. After this, the essay then runs down the fish's spine, with each of the ribs representing different sections replete with analysis, where you go into an important issue or question that needs critical discussion to achieve your overall argument. In all these different sections of discussion, you are remaining within the bounds of the spine and overall direction of the essay: you are not leaping off to a random topic that does not fit or follow sequentially in the order of things. This all runs through to the tail, being your *conclusion* that ties up your findings and discusses useful implications of them *moving forward*.

Can you pause for a moment and work out the most important element in this fish skeleton?

6. Structure

That's right: the *spine!* This is the backbone of your essay, where you have a clear and consistent narrative running throughout. Matters are all dealt with in a logical sequence and all matters are concluded in a way that supports the overarching direction and theme of the essay. Related to the need for the spine to have a clear running sequence and logical order is the need for careful and strategic design of all the different sections of analysis, as covered in the previous chapter. Not only does this sequencing refer to the main sections within your essay, but in fact every paragraph or area of discussion. It thus means careful strategic design of paragraphs and sentences, to ensure that they have a clear purpose and are developed in a clear, coherent and logical sequence.

The fish spine analogy also corresponds nicely with another analogy used for essay structure, which is the diamond structure:

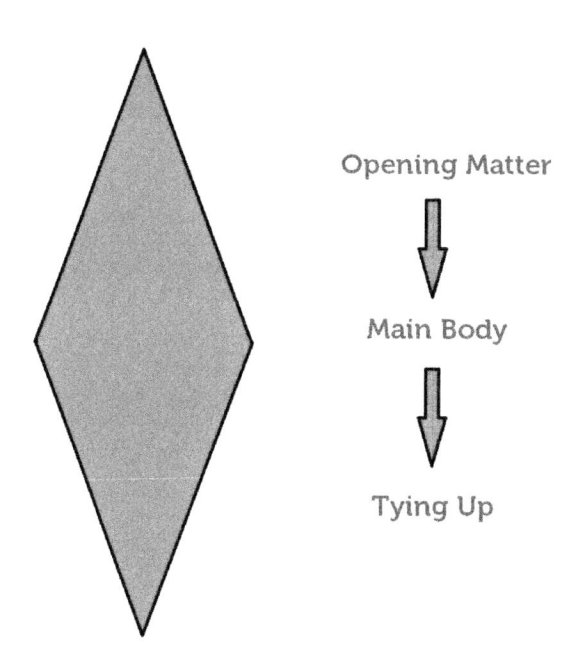

Opening Matter

⬇

Main Body

⬇

Tying Up

Diamond Essay Structure
Image Credit: Author's Own

113

The diamond structure reminds students that an essay needs to be a coherent whole, where the threads and discussions raised in the beginning need to be carried through into the analysis in the main body. Importantly, it also emphasizes that all these ideas and concepts need to be "tied up". It therefore reminds us that we need to make sure that there is a clear journey through the essay and that there should not be random ideas or discussions that take us too far from the journey towards the conclusion. I still prefer the fish skeleton, as I think it encapsulates this and emphasizes other components, such as the inner ribs of analysis and the central spine.

Ultimately, it is clear to your marker when a piece of work has been produced as a "stream of consciousness" that is just bashed out on to the page in one or two takes. The best pieces of work require a lot of strategic and careful planning, with a lot of moving and shifting of different discussions, along with some prior planning about what comes where in the essay journey.

2. Signposting and Signalling

Powerful structure is therefore about effective **signposting** and **signalling**. I often say that you have got to "hold the reader's hand through the journey." It needs to form a coherent *whole* throughout, where the reader is aware, at every stage, about the journey that they are moving through. Imagine that your reader is walking through woodland and you need to highlight the route with occasional signposts and signals. They need to be able to reasonably anticipate what is coming up next or understand why their walk is going down certain paths.

Signposts and signals should be present throughout your essay. They may summarize the findings drawn from key sections or begin a section by explaining or justifying its aims. Your introduction and conclusion are key signposts. The introduction really maps out the journey ahead and explains the aims, focus and direction of the essay, as well as the stops along the way. The conclusion similarly summarizes what has been discovered along our woodland walk and what it all means. Ultimately, the reader needs to understand how all the discussions and points link together and how they all fit within a sequence running down the fish's spine.

There can also be simple signals in the words, to provide clues as to links between concepts and ideas, or to signify a change in direction or a further step in the discussion. This linking or "transition" language in essays makes a huge difference to helping readers understand the flow and direction of the narrative, as well as understanding the links between ideas being discussed. It is quite often referred to as the "thread" that runs through your essay, because it is like a rope handrail that the reader holds onto from start to finish. Look at the following table which has been adapted from a table developed by Queen's University Belfast. The words in the second column can be incredibly helpful for linking between ideas and discussions in the narrative of your essay. They are "transition" phrases and they link discussions together or provide sequences along the thread in your running narrative.

Linking Signal	Useful Words and Phrases
To add more ideas	*Furthermore, In addition, Moreover, Similarly, Also, On the whole, Likewise, In the same way, Equally, Another*
To compare or contrast ideas	*Alternatively, Contrastingly, Conversely, Whereas, By contrast, An exception to this is*
To prove something	*Evidently, For this reason, Because, Inevitably, Correspondingly, As such*

To show exceptions	However, Nevertheless, Yet, In spite of, Despite this, On the other hand
To repeat or refer back to something	As has been mentioned, As noted earlier, As previously discussed, As highlighted above, Again
To note something coming later	As will be discussed later
To emphasise something	Definitely, Obviously, Inevitably, Undeniably
To express a caution or condition	Unless, Provided that, If, As long as, This requires
To give an example	For instance, For example, This can be seen in, As demonstrated by
To show the order of things	Previously, Following this, Initially, Subsequently, Finally, Regarding, In conclusion
To go deeper into something	Thus, Therefore, Accordingly, Because of this, As a result, In effect, Consequently

Your essay title and the headings of your sections are also key signposts for the reader. Say you have a section titled "3. Game Theoretical Analysis of Self-Managed Teams". This signifies quite clearly that the section will provide a game theoretical analysis of self-managed teams! We can expect that section to remain on topic and to draw a helpful conclusion from the analysis that supports the overarching theme and direction of the essay. It is worth also noting that that you may not need to call your first and last sections just "Introduction" and "Conclusion". You can use the headings as an opportunity to further communicate what the focus of the section is using a colon (:). For example,

"Introduction: The Need for Sociological Insights into Online Gambling" and "Conclusion: Future Demographical Analyses of Gambling Addiction". This is not a requirement, but it's an idea that can be helpful to improve your overall communication to yourself and the reader.

Another common form of signposting therefore is the use of *lists*. For example, *"There are several reasons for this. Firstly, …. Secondly, …. Finally, there is also…."* Your reader can easily follow this discussion thread, as you tick through each item in the list. Your signposting and signalling throughout the essay can be subtle and concise in its use of words. Avoid being too detailed in signalling to the reader unless you feel it is absolutely necessary to prevent the reader getting lost. It just needs to be enough to link from one issue/idea/concept to the next. There is more on this when we come to Concise Writing in Chapter 8.

3. Paragraph Structuring

Paragraphs are such an important and underappreciated aspect of essay structuring. I have come across too many essays with lots of single sentences for paragraphs or, worse, where paragraphs are a page long. Using paragraphs effectively makes your essay much more digestible and enjoyable. It also does an excellent job of demarcating issues into "steps", so that your reader can comfortably follow the journey as if they are walking along steppingstones organized in a neat, straight line.

A common question from students is how long paragraphs should be. It is a good question because it is hard to ever be too precise or prescriptive with an answer. In general, one would expect paragraphs to be somewhere between 6-12 lines in length. They need to be sufficiently long to cover enough detail; and sufficiently short to be easy on the eye. It can require a bit of moving and shifting to get things neatly expressed within neat "blocks" like this, calling for some careful and clever manoeuvring. Sometimes you need to split something up into two paragraphs or you might need to conjoin two points together in a paragraph with a "pivot" in the middle: such as a change of direction mid-paragraph, using words like "However" or "By contrast". It also forces you to choose words carefully and to ensure matters are being dealt with concisely, so that everything fits together as neatly as possible.

Topic Sentences

Students rarely appreciate the power of topic sentences. That, by the way, was a topic sentence. It sets the scene for the coming paragraph and signposts to the reader what the focus of the paragraph will be. It serves as an anchor around which the following body of analysis will be related. It might signal a change in direction of your argument, or it may be opening a new line of analysis or exploring a counter-perspective. In most cases, the topic sentence will be at the beginning of the paragraph. Less commonly, they may appear in the second sentence, such as when the first one is linking to the previous paragraph or is providing important information to contextualize the topic sentence that follows.

You could also have a second topic sentence within a paragraph, to show a strong pivot in the direction of the argument mid-paragraph, such as opening a counter-perspective. This is possible given that a paragraph should be a standalone section of discussion or analysis. If that analysis calls for a change of direction, then it is possible to pivot the direction mid-paragraph. However (note the pivot here!), it is important that pivots mid-paragraph are easy to identify and make sense. Use clear terms to contrast the discussion from what has just been said, such as "However", "Despite this" or "By contrast". Also, do not say pivoting transitions like these and then follow with a statement that does not clearly detract away the preceding discussion!

Topic sentences are often short and punchy. That said, it can be wearisome to repeat the same style of topic sentence and might be good to "mix it up" with some that are more complex or longer sentences. The main point is that you are always signalling the analysis that is to follow, helping the reader to know where in the journey you are taking them next.

Avoid over-using questions as topic sentences, which is something that many students do. Asking questions is a little informal, or even condescending, in tone. It also wastes words. For example, starting with, "What, then, is the solution to this problem?" or "Are there any weaknesses in the theory propounded by Miller et al?" It is great to be asking these questions, as they help *you* define the focus of the next paragraph. They are a wonderful example of you anticipating what the reader should be asking. However, rephrase them as positive statements. For example, "One widely promoted solution to this problem is the adoption of…" or "However, there are several weaknesses with Miller et al's theory." These are great topic sentences that immediately signal to the reader the discussions to come.

PEAL

Paragraphs need to be developed as a coherent whole. Many have even referred to the idea of seeing paragraphs as mini-essays that have a topic sentence as an introduction, then explain the point or raise evidence, then undertake analysis or discussion, before then finally concluding. Their structure has even been associated with the "diamond" structure of essays, discussed above, where matters are opened at the beginning, expanded in the middle, and tied up at the end.

In fact, there is no set way to structure a paragraph: it is solely about having a clear and coherent narrative that is easy for the reader to follow and navigate, however one achieves it. Nevertheless, a common structural template that many promote is the acronym PEAL or PEEL. I prefer the PEAL acronym, interpreted in the following way:

POINT	This is effectively like your topic sentence. It signals to the reader what the focus or overall point of this section of analysis will be.
EXPLANATION EVIDENCE EXAMPLE	This explains what the issue is or provides evidence of the problem.
ANALYSIS	The main body of the discussion where you undertake critical analysis of the issue and develop your *argument* in response.
LINK	Links your analysis back to the overall argument. Shows relevance of preceding discussion to the journey down the fish's spine.

Look at the following paragraph as an example (taken from my paper on community governance, published in *Transnational Environmental Law*):

Achieving community buy-in is essential to achieve all forms of natural and cultural heritage protection. The resources, tools, daily engagement, and close proximity of local communities makes them truly invaluable as "partners" in the protection of our global heritage.[35] In the context of archaeological resources, examples continuously arise of more effective heritage management through collaboration with local communities.[36] By its capacity to make integrated use of traditional practices, knowledge, and innovation, such public-private integration also has numerous social benefits and puts a much greater value on cultural and indigenous diversity. While stakeholder-led governance can take more time and effort to reach agreed rules, the resulting quality of the norms and the high level of community buy-in make the overall implementation far more time-efficient and more effective overall.[37]

If we analyze this paragraph from a PEAL perspective, we can see that the opening sentence is a topic sentence. It indicates the *point* of the paragraph (about the importance of community buy-in when achieving community governance). The next sentence *explains* that further or *adds evidence* of the point being made. It is significant, for example, that it has a footnote referencing evidence to back up the point being established.

The next two sentences and the beginning of the final sentence provide further *analysis* or application of that point, highlighting potential benefits and drawbacks. The second half of the final sentence provides a useful conclusion for that paragraph. In effect, it says that despite some challenges (around time and effort), the benefits of achieving community governance far outweigh the drawbacks. It helps *link* it all together by setting up the discussion to follow in the next paragraph in the journey, which goes into deeper analysis on the challenges of achieving effective community governance. See here:

Example PEAL Paragraph

POINT	*Achieving community buy-in is essential to achieve all forms of natural and cultural heritage protection.*
EXPLANATION / EVIDENCE	*The resources, tools, daily engagement, and close proximity of local communities makes them truly invaluable as "partners" in the protection of our global heritage.*[35]

ANALYSIS   *In the context of archaeological resources, examples continuously arise of more effective heritage management through collaboration with local communities.[36] By its capacity to make integrated use of traditional practices, knowledge, and innovation, such public-private integration also has numerous social benefits and puts a much greater value on cultural and indigenous diversity. While stakeholder-led governance can take more time and effort to reach agreed rules,*

LINK   *the resulting quality of the norms and the high level of community buy-in make the overall implementation far more time-efficient and more effective overall.[37]*

I am not personally wedded to the PEAL structure. The reality is that paragraphs come in many types and varieties, without all fitting neatly into this four-part structure. Nevertheless, many students find it helpful as a reminder to consider the "journey" through a paragraph.

The point is simply to be aware that paragraphs need to be meaty enough to thoroughly address, analyze or explain a particular point and they need to reach some kind of conclusion or resolution. If they are unresolved, then the following paragraph *must* be a continuation of the analysis, until the discussion reaches an unambiguous conclusion. Paragraphs also need to have a clear focus, which can be readily discerned by the reader within the first line; and the reader needs to feel like they have resolved something or taken a step forward by the paragraph's end.

In terms of broader paragraph structure, compare the next two paragraphs. The paragraph in question is adapted from Alan Durant and Nigel Fabb (2005) *How to Write Essays and Dissertations: A Guide for English Literature Students*, Taylor & Francis Group. The first paragraph is the "messed up" version, where sentences have been moved around. The second paragraph is the original paragraph, put back in the proper order:

> We end by showing how suitably chosen combinations of essay focus and mode of argument can create coherent overall projects. In this unit, we work through two related processes: (i) narrowing down the topic, and (ii) imposing a structure on your treatment of that topic. But, if you have a free choice of topic, you will be setting your own question and need to work out how to approach it for yourself. When you answer a set question it is essential to think about exactly what kind of question you are answering and approach the topic accordingly.

As compared with:

> When you answer a set question it is essential to think about exactly what kind of question you are answering and approach the topic accordingly. But, if you have a free choice of topic, you will be setting your own question and need to work out how to approach it for yourself. In this unit, we work through two related processes: (i) narrowing down the topic, and (ii) imposing a structure on your treatment of that topic. We end by showing how suitably chosen combinations of essay focus and mode of argument can create coherent overall projects.

After a simple rearrangement from the original, the "disordered" paragraph becomes incredibly difficult to follow, with its meaning almost entirely obscured. Such messy paragraphs are *exactly* the kind of problem we see too often in poorly structured work. It is evidence of a student who is waffling, instead of carefully planning their work. The main thing is ensuring that the discussion is linear and is introducing matters and tying them up, as it works through a series of steps. Each step is adding one small component on top of the structure that is being built: much like building a tower, one brick at a time.

Concluding Sentences

Just as you need topic sentences to signal the opening of a discussion, you also need to bring such discussions to clear conclusion, whatever that conclusion may be. I find that effective concluding sentences are an often undervalued and underutilized tool by students. Too often I read sections of discussion that suddenly end without me having any idea what the conclusion or finding was. You should therefore ensure that the reader is always able to grasp what has been concluded or discovered from a preceding analysis. Many have suggested that a concluding sentence can serve as a response to the question, "So what?" Having taken together all the discussions and points in the preceding discussion, where does this leave us? How is this valuable? How does it link back to the main thread or argument?

However, as noted above, not every paragraph needs a concluding sentence. It could be that the following paragraph is a natural continuation of the discussion from the previous paragraph. In some cases, the findings of the paragraph might be obvious, such that no "conclusion" is needed. (In effect, no further sentence is needed either, as the paragraph has done its job!) Or, if the analysis findings come across clearly and succinctly, you may also simply use the following paragraph's topic sentence to draw upon the previous paragraph's conclusion. For example, a topic sentence might start, "*While the KISS principle presents numerous advantages for coders, there are numerous risks inherent from the perspective of the app user.*" This serves as both a conclusion of the preceding paragraph (that it carries advantages) and a topic sentence for what is to follow (about risks for the app user).

6. Structure

Once again there are no hard rules on how to write or use concluding sentences or concluding components within a section. It is just important to ensure that threads of discussion do not suddenly end in a way that the reader cannot easily discern what has been discovered. I therefore disagree with those who say that a sentence is needed at the end that ensures we have "moved on" from the topic sentence. Sometimes the preceding topic sentence can even act as our concluding sentence! Just make sure when reading back that threads are clearly tied up or the "So what?" is easy for the reader to discern.

Word Count

I have some critically important advice around your management of any maximum word counts:

- ✓ **Use all the available word count**

I have had hundreds of students ask me whether they need to use up the available word count. The answer is always the same: yes. If a student does not use up the available word count, it means two things. Firstly, it means they have not done hardly enough work on their essay or enough research. *It is possible to write an entire book on any essay question.* So, if you are only using 70% of the available words, then you are clearly not doing enough. Anyone who has done their homework or who has developed a rich and detailed knowledge on the topic will be bursting at the seams with things to talk about; and the maximum word limit would inevitably be too tight.

Secondly, that student has not maximized the opportunity to demonstrate evidence of meeting the assessment criteria. If you are trying to evidence your knowledge and understanding, your ability to comprehend wider materials, and your ability to structure a comprehensive argument, then make use of all available words to show this. As such, you want to be aiming to be within a few words of the maximum word count, as this suggests you were bursting with ideas and had to refine them to fit all your ideas in. At a minimum, it should be above 95% of the available space.

✓ **Do not exceed the maximum word count**
On the flip side, you must **never** exceed the maximum word count. Using modern tools and technology, it is easy for your tutors to verify that you have not exceeded the word count. We impose word counts for a number of reasons, but the main one is to get you practising the skills of being concise and to compress all your arguments and points into a clear, effective and brief expression. It also means we can assess all students equally. It also shows a lack of care and a lack of attention-to-detail when we are assessing a student's abilities to follow the brief. We therefore impose strict penalties for exceeding the word count. Just don't do it. It is always possible to revise, reformulate and condense your arguments to fit within the available space. If you have too much, you may need to omit ideas and sections, or just continue condensing. But you will get there.

✓ **Pay close attention to what is included and excluded in the word count**
Different courses and universities have different expectations about what is included, be it titles, footnotes, bibliographies, references, tables, image caption, abstracts and so on. They also have different rules around whether the word count stated is the upper limit or can be exceeded by a certain percentage. Be sure to observe those rules closely. When checking your word count, ensure you highlight the relevant sections if calculating based on different components together. Similarly, if using footnotes and these are excluded, make sure to tick the option under the 'Word Count' tab to 'Exclude footnotes and endnotes'.

4. Sentence Structuring

Effective sentence writing also forms an aspect of structure. If sentences are all back-to-front, do not have a clear focus, or seemingly never end, they will make the essay messy, erratic, and hard to follow. Effective writing and sentence layout

6. Structure

is more closely associated with having good grammar and syntax and so is explored in much greater detail in Chapter 8 on Writing. As discussed there, one of the most common structural errors I see in student writing is sentence *fragments* and *run-on*. This means, in effect, that sentences are incomplete or should have finished sooner. Ensuring your sentences are appropriately structured, have a clear single point and are of a suitable and digestible length, will all serve to significantly improve your essay's structure.

That said, there are a few specific tips and tricks of sentence building that you can use to strengthen your essay's structure:

✓ **Make strategic use of *italics***

Occasionally a sentence comes along which benefits from a word or phrase being italicized, like *this*. This might be necessary to ensure the sentence has the appropriate meaning or ensure that the reader places stress or particular note on the *keyword*. It is important not to over-do the use of italics however: too much changing of formats will make the work look messy and erratic.

✓ **Become proficient in the use of punctuation**

One of the most common issues I see with student writing is the misuse and muddled application of punctuation. Punctuation—with its driving influence on the speed, direction, emphasis and meaning of written language—is an essential component of good essay structure. Spend a lot of time observing written communication that has accurate and effective use of punctuation. Make particular note of the use of commas, periods, dashes, colons, brackets and semicolons. These tools can be essential in controlling the flow, rhythm and focus of the reader. See more in Chapter 8.

✓ **Try to make sure each sentence has one clear point**

As noted, one of the most common issues with sentence structuring is sentence run-on, where a sentence continues running when it should have stopped or had a conjunction. I need to remind students not to be afraid of full stops. Relatedly, it is helpful to ensure that each sentence has one clear point it is making. If it has more than one pivot or transition (e.g., *however, that said, nevertheless, also, furthermore, as well as*, etc), then it is trying to cover too much. Using more direct and punchy sentences will ensure that points come across with the greatest level of clarity.

✓ **Consider the average reading voice and rhythm**

This is a tricky one, but when proofreading or editing your work, consider the average reader. What speed would they be reading when they are in full flow? What might cause them to get stuck or suddenly trip up with the language? Where might they be reading too quickly that they lose track of what is being said or run out of breath? When reading back your work, gently read it with the speed, rhythm and tone of someone with a calm, confident and comfortable grasp of English literacy. It might help to listen to your work being narrated by the computer voice in an application like Word. When listening, you want to imagine it's an audiobook and it's important for listeners to easily follow along. Does it suddenly go too fast in certain places? Does it break the flow or sound weird when pauses suddenly come in? Is emphasis being lost on key points? The more you read with an awareness of these points, the more your own writing will improve.

✓ **Observe the common thread**

A key component of good essay structure, as symbolized with the fish spine earlier, is the common thread running through the entire essay. This is the running narrative that unfolds the story, in your own academic voice. Make sure that everything is tethered to this common thread. This relates particularly to the skilful and strategic use of transition phrases and words, *as discussed above*.

Ensure that the direction and flow of your discussion is clearly signalled by these transitional phrases. This could include the skilful use of lists, where you might use transitional phrases like *Firstly, Secondly, Thirdly*, and *Finally*. They all keep everything neatly tied back to the fish spine.

✓ **Avoid descriptive or "walk-through" transitional phrases**

As stressed in Chapter 3, it is fundamentally important to emphasize argument or analysis, and to avoid descriptive writing. Using certain "walk-through" transitional phrases could be indicative of descriptive writing. A common example is when time-related transition phrases are used (e.g., *first, next, then, after that, following this*) or certain listing phrases e.g., (*also, in addition, another*). These can be effective in analytical discourse but are most commonly seen in descriptive accounts that only explain what has happened, rather than evaluating what this means.

✓ **Read Chapters 8 and 9**

In fact, reading this whole book will improve your essay structure! However, in the context of building your essay out of grammatically arranged words and sentences, I stress the need to also read Chapter 8 on Writing and 9 on Writing Approaches. They highlight extremely common errors and issues with student writing on essays, with lots of tips and guidance on addressing them. Improving the quality and execution of your writing makes your essay much easier to read, gives it a better flow, makes it more reliable and professional in tone, and helps keep your reader engaged and connected to the essay's journey.

7. Introduction and Conclusion

1. How to Write an Introduction

I have heard many professors say they can immediately tell what grade a paper will get within the first two lines. They are not kidding. I know because I can often do the same. There is a reason why thousands of students take to the internet every year to ask how to write the perfect introduction for an essay. This section gets straight to the point and tells you everything you need to know. It explains what to include in an introduction and how to get it right, every time.

Introduction Length
Let us first be sure here that we are talking about a traditional "essay" assignment. For some assignments, such as direct question-and-answer exercises or problem scenarios, you may have different instructions or may even be expected to dispense with the introduction altogether and go straight into your answer. Similarly, some assignments—such as oral presentations, letter writing or report writing—may have slightly different expectations in terms of introductions.

If we are talking about the standard academic essay assignment, then the general rule of thumb is that the introduction is roughly around 10% of the word count. It is sometimes expressed as somewhere between 5-15% and, certainly, you should use your own judgement as to what is an appropriate length depending on the nature of the paper. However, 10% is perhaps a suitable target to have in mind. For a short essay of 1,000 words, this is likely to equate to a short paragraph comprising 3 or 4 sentences. For a 15,000-word dissertation, this is likely to consist of a chapter close to 1,500 words.

What Goes in an Introduction

Mapping out an excellent introduction is pretty simple and requires only four key components. Despite its simplicity, so many students continuously fail to cover these four elements or fail to cover them in a clear, concise and sufficiently detailed manner.

The four components your introduction needs are:

1	IMPORTANCE OF SUBJECT	The subject of the paper and why it's an important, interesting or engaging topic.
2	CURRENT THINKING	Concise expression of the key current thinking/debates on the subject.
3	ARGUMENT	The argument of the paper.
4	ROADMAP	How the argument will be conducted. In other words, a map of the essay's journey.

Let's open these up:

1) The subject of the paper and why it's important

This is your opening few sentences where you immediately hit the reader with the subject matter at the centre of the paper and why the topic is important or interesting. It is about grabbing the reader's attention and immediately situating them in the "problem" or subject of discussion. Is it a controversial or uncertain area? Has there been a lot of research and a lack of answers? Is there a strong public interest?

Example (adapted from Plass, J.L. and Kalyuga, S. (2019) 'Four Ways of Considering Emotion in Cognitive Load Theory', *Educational Psychology Review* 31 339-359):

"*Cognitive Load Theory (CLT) has become one of the most dominant learning theories in educational psychology. First developed in the 1980s (Sweller 1988), CLT is highly popular with practitioners on account of its useful and concrete predictions and prescriptions in instructional design.*"

As you can see, you want to hit the reader straight away and "situate" them in the theme of the paper. It needs to be a concise expression about the critical topic under focus for the paper. You then need to highlight the importance of the topic. In doing so, it can sometimes be good in the lines following to refer to significant statistics or to use a powerful quote, to hit the point home or emphasize the subject's importance. Some examples might include:

- *This has been described as one of commercial arbitration's most challenging issues*[1] *where "Most relevant questions, including notion, relevance and applicability are not settled."*[2]

- *According to estimates, 29% of Leave voters are beginning to express Brexit regret, or "Bregret" (Pullman 2021).*

2) A concise expression of the current thinking/debate on the subject

After grabbing the reader's attention and alerting them to the subject matter, you now need to contextualize the discussions in your paper by briefly summarizing some of the current thinking or studies related to your core question. What are the key arguments or evidential findings in this field and why is there still a gap in these? What are the current theories or ideas, related to your argument, that are being discussed? What is the crux of the debate and where do present academics sit on the spectrum?

In many ways, you want to be imagining that this component will be followed by a statement saying, in effect, "This essay therefore contributes to *this* discussion by arguing…".

Example:
"The theory's significance is in part because it is grounded in understanding the human cognitive architecture that is supported by decades of research on working memory models (Baddeley 1986; Cowan 2001), schema construction (McVee et al. 2005; Paas et al. 2004), and mental effort (Salomon 1984). CLT is continuing to evolve by incorporating new theoretical insights from these and other areas (Plass et al. 2010)."

3) The argument of the paper

Many students mistakenly believe that the argument or findings of their paper should be a mystery, kept hidden from the reader throughout the essay, until magically unveiled at the end to the relief of the reader. This approach is seemingly indoctrinated in students at school or pre-university education but is completely incorrect at university level and beyond. In academic writing, your arguments and findings are the *most central and critical component of your paper*. It is crucial that you indicate the position or argument of the paper in the introduction, allowing the reader to know what the paper is seeking to persuade them of.

An academic paper should be carrying out critical discussions, with reference to evidence, to persuade the readers of your hypothesis. In the social sciences and humanities, it is more common for written work to centre on the development of an argument with reference to critical analysis and evidence. In STEM-oriented disciplines, it is more common that a paper will set out a research question and then conduct primary and secondary research to present new findings, and then will interpret those findings and draw conclusions. The paper's introduction should still, in either case, signal to the reader what the overall argument or findings of the paper are. Make that clear from the outset and do not make it a mystery. This not only helps the reader to understand your whole essay, but also helps *you* to be clear and focused on the essay's primary objective from start to finish.

Example:
"This essay argues that affective processing, and especially a learner's emotional experiences during learning, has not yet been sufficiently considered in the context of CLT (Brünken et al. 2010). It suggests that a comprehensive understanding of cognitive processing requires the consideration of affective factors related to the experience of feeling or emotion."

4) How the argument will be conducted

The last part of your introduction should briefly summarize how you are going to proceed in your paper, discussing its general layout in a succinct and direct manner. It is a very brief and concise layout of the paper's order of argumentation or analysis sequencing (see Chapter 5). You might also highlight the key evidence you will be using or what kind of methodology you are using, if these are noteworthy. All of this helps signal to the reader how the paper will make its argument or answer its question. It also improves the readability of the whole paper, as the reader has been given clues about the different stops on the journey.

You may also want to add some insights into what your findings are or what the implications of them could be. Have you discovered that there still remain gaps or uncertainties? Has your paper discovered the main grounds on which to sustain your core argument? Has your paper drawn out some important implications of this argument? Have your research findings established a potentially new insight? You only need to provide a short teaser of things like this for now, to intrigue the reader; you will properly expand on them in your subsequent discussions and conclusions. The key is being super concise in explaining the key checkpoints along the journey coming up.

Example:
"The essay will first define CLT and describe various recent refinements, before describing how processing models of multimedia learning have incorporated affect and the inclusion of emotion, motivation, and meta-cognition (Moreno and Mayer 2007). It then summarizes research on emotion and cognition, and on learning and emotion, before concluding with four ways in which emotion relates to cognitive load."

These four different components will usually come in that order: starting with 1 and ending with 4. However, it is possible to see them in different orders, if the introduction still has a logical flow and communicates the points in a clear, thoughtful and engaging way. It certainly might make sense to keep the first component—introducing the general subject matter of the paper and its importance—first. Whenever you are reading peer-reviewed articles or exemplar essays, start looking out for these four components in the introduction. You will usually be able to find all four in most cases, depending on the context of the paper or the quality of the essay. In doing so, make a note of how they are connected. While you are at it, go back to the first paragraph in this chapter too, for another example!

Making it a Perfect Introduction

Now you know the four components to a perfect essay introduction, the next thing is how to get it just right. It might be stating the obvious, but you should be proofreading your work constantly. It is good to take occasional breaks from writing new things and to instead go back over your writing in progress, addressing areas where the writing does not flow well or feels jumbled. While doing this, you can also fix typos, cut down extraneous words and generally perfect the quality of your delivery. Given the critical importance of having a solid introduction to your essay, you ideally should have reviewed and improved the introduction a few times by the end.

One of the tricky aspects of a good introduction is the need to use super concise writing. Covering these four components in a way that is clear, content-rich and engaging, while also using a small number of words, is a challenge. Therefore, review Chapter 9 for more detailed guidance on writing concisely.

You might sometimes hear it being suggested that you should write your introduction last. So the thinking goes: given that the introduction is setting out what is to come, you need to know what is to come before you can set it out. I urge a strong word of caution with this. If you do not know roughly what the essay is likely to say before you embark on the essay, then you have already set yourself up to fail. A good essay is all about planning and having a reasonably clear idea of the structure before writing it. You should ideally be able to at least draft a rough introduction, subject to later change and refinement, to help set the context and aims of your essay. Or, at the very least, have an introduction made up on bullet points, as a prompt to its likely contents. Doing this will help *you* by making you concisely express the overall aims of the paper and its general direction, before you then set out to achieve that.

As discussed in Chapter 8, a key part of effective writing is *conscious reading*. Using this, observe how effective introductions are written by others across the wider literature. When reading academic articles, take a note of the four components (subject, research context, argument, and structure of paper) and look at the different approaches and styles. Also, make sure that your opening few sentences hit the mark perfectly. You must avoid any typos or writing weaknesses in the first few lines.

Finally, I must advise against defining all your key terms in the introduction. For certain, you need to explain the subject of the paper and its context. However, do not waste words in the introduction providing lots of background definitions which are not integrated into the main flow of discussion. You can explain and define matters as they come up in the essay. Reserve the introduction for a concise, powerful statement on the *whole* subject area, thesis aims and essay roadmap.

2. How to Write a Conclusion

A question I have been asked all too often in my years of mentoring thousands of students with their essays is "*What is the difference between an introduction and conclusion?*" It is understandable that the two appear largely similar. Surely, they *both* just summarize your key arguments and findings, right? Not at all. The situation is not helped by the poor advice I frequently see circulating on the internet, telling students: "Say what you are going to say. Say it. Then, say it again." That is terrible advice. While being clear on your arguments and signposting ideas throughout your paper is essential, there is no room to waste words on just repeating ourselves.

Your conclusion is absolutely not a repetition of your introduction. It brings together the *detail* from all your findings and arguments throughout the essay into a concise summary, with all of it angled towards *persuading* the reader of your overall arguments. Whereas the introduction serves as a signalling device, giving a general clue about what is to come; the conclusion is based on referring back to and building upon the *actual findings* throughout the essay. It is also an opportunity to highlight the implications of these findings: not just what we have discovered, but *what does this mean*? What are the potential future implications, applications or challenges that can be drawn from our findings?

The truth is that there is no correct way or standard template for a conclusion. The most important function of the conclusion is assisting the reader in drawing together a clear picture of everything that can be taken away from the paper. It also should finish in a nice rounded way, with your last passage really punching with force, flourish and finesse. It should leave the reader with a good last impression of the paper and perhaps even important questions or ideas to ponder. Again, it is also good to closely observe academic articles and exemplar essays to spot the features and components of strong concluding sections.

While there is no set template on what goes in your conclusion, the following are a series of questions for you to consider when drawing together your conclusion:

- *What picture emerges when we pull all of the essay's findings together?*
- *What significant or useful findings or conclusions have been established?*
- *What are key solutions or hypotheses that might be used to respond to the core findings?*
- *What are potential future applications or implications of the findings?*
- *What are some future questions or debates that may emerge from the findings?*

In addition, here are additional super useful tips and pointers on writing excellent conclusions:

✓ **Aim for your conclusion to be around 5-10% of the word count**

Like with the introduction, you want to picture around 10% of your word count being used on the conclusion. In fact, given that the conclusion is just tying things up and is not going back into issues, it can sometimes be shorter than the introduction (down to 5%). It is quality, not quantity. If it is useful, informative and adeptly pulls all the threads together, then it does not need to use up masses of space.

✓ Do not just describe what has been discussed

Avoid conclusions that just plod back through the essay, describing the journey that is just been taken. We know what we have looked at, but we need to see a picture of what *it all means* when we tie it together. Therefore, avoid conclusions that say things like, "Next the paper looked at this. Then it looked at that. Then it established that. Finally, it discussed this." This is only repeating what has happened and we already know that. Think more about what all of *this* and *that* mean when taken *together*. It is about pulling together all the threads of discussion from the paper and knitting them into a pretty, little patchwork. You can certainly remind the reader of key findings from the paper, but weave this into the concluding analysis, rather than just repeating it all again in an automated manner.

✓ Take the opportunity to rephrase and reframe findings

Conclusions provide a useful opportunity to rephrase and reframe your findings. For example, try not to repeat your findings using the same words and phrases that were used in the main body. Changing the way you express your findings and ideas not only helps to keep the essay engaging, but also helps the reader to understand them better.

✓ Think of the reader

The conclusion is an essential aspect of essay structuring, enabling the reader to have the key findings, hypotheses or overall implications firmly in mind by the end. Consider the journey the reader has been on and whether there are any complex areas that might need rephrasing or summarizing again. Consider whether there are any questions from the reader that might be left unanswered. If there are, then of course it might indicate that you need to do some further work and refinement on the main body of the paper. However, it might be a matter that can be succinctly addressed as part of the concluding discussions.

7. Introduction and Conclusion

✓ **Think of the future**

As mentioned, it is all very well just drawing together all the threads of the paper to formulate a picture of what has been discovered, but it is really about what that picture *means*. Therefore, instead of seeing the conclusion as solely backward focused (looking back at what has been discussed), make sure it focuses on the future too (what this all means for the future). As noted, what are useful or interesting approaches, solutions, debates, applications, insights or ideas that might emerge? What might future research in this field want to examine? How has the paper hopefully contributed to the debate outlined at the beginning?

✓ **Avoid introducing new analyses**

Some academics suggest that your conclusion should not contain any new evidence, materials or questions. It should purely be used to draw together what has been discussed. I again express caution on taking this too literally. If there is any evidence, materials or questions that relate specifically to the conclusion and the future implications of the paper's findings, then put them in! For example, if you are saying that the findings might contribute to a debate that is been asked in another part of your subject's discipline, do not be afraid to drop some references in to allude to this debate! I think the important thing though—and what these academics really mean—is that you need to be focused on concluding and tying up the paper, instead of moving *back* into the issues and questions that *should have been* addressed in the main body. But making allusions to wider evidence that relates *specifically to your conclusion* is a good thing.

✓ **Do not conclude at a position that is not discussed or analyzed in your essay**

Another very common weakness is the arrival of an unforeseen conclusion, from out of nowhere, that is not a logical ending to the preceding analyses and discussions. A common cause of this is when a student suddenly shoehorns an answer to the assignment brief into their conclusion but has failed to answer the brief in the main body. Your closing elements need to serve as a natural and logical conclusion to what has already been discussed. It is fine to discuss what the implications of your findings are, with further insights not previously discussed, but make sure that is all still feeding off a logical and coherent conclusion to previous discussions.

✓ **Make sure that your conclusion or overall argument still hits the brief.**

It was mentioned in Chapter 2 that you want to go back to your assessment instructions several times in the essay process to double-check you are still addressing the question. An important time to do that is when you are concluding your essay and tying up all the threads and discussions. If it is not quite fitting the brief, then it is perhaps your essay that needs tweaking, rather than the conclusion!

✓ **Do not apologize!**

I have graded many papers where student states in their conclusion words to the effect of, "Sorry this essay was not as good as I am usually capable of." Such apologies might be more subtle, saying things like, "However, this paper was only able to focus on this [less significant] point". Or it says words like, "Given more time and preparation, this paper could have explored the more important questions", or "This is just one answer and there are certainly better ones." Leave anything like this out. Use positive language and speak positively about what you have discovered, even if it is not as impressive or extensive as you had originally hoped. (You never know; the marker might actually be super impressed with it!)

That said, it is perfectly okay to define the parameters of the paper and acknowledge questions or debates that have not been addressed. But avoid doing this in an apologetic manner at the end. You are trying to leave a positive note in the reader's mind about the paper's utility and application. If needed, state the parameters of the paper in a positive tone and earlier on, perhaps when defining the field of enquiry or not long after your introduction.

- ✓ **Finish with a powerful last sentence**

It might sound obvious, but so many people do not stop and think about it. Just as your first sentence is super important, so is your final sentence. It is your signature on the paper and the final words that the reader will take away with them. You can even afford to be sensationalist or slightly dramatic. Certainly, there is no harm using a bit of flourish or flavourful language. Make it interesting. Leave them thinking or pondering something. Give them a slogan to take away. And, above all else, make sure the final sentence is well constructed, flows nicely and is free from errors!

For what it is worth, I include some of the last sentences in my own academic papers:

➢ *"If we are ever to govern this blue planet effectively, a transnational law of the sea is not just desirable—it is indispensable."* (NB: 'Transnational Law of the Sea' was the title of the paper.)

➢ *"In so doing, we could expand the global protection of [Underwater Cultural Heritage] by truly unleashing the power of the community."*

➢ *"All of this would resolve the core weakness right at the heart of the UK's policy, which appears to propagate the wisdom that [Underwater Cultural Heritage] is merely an obstacle or pathway to economic advancement, rather than a fundamentally important public resource for perpetual research, remembrance, identity, communal engagement and social fulfilment."*

➢ "The first port of call in such negotiations would be to scrap the tainted International Titanic Agreement and to launch new international negotiations towards a more integrated, inclusive, visionary and conservation-minded [Marine Protected Area] which finally protects the world's most beloved shipwreck for future generations."

➢ "Perhaps our only choice remains 'rough justice – or no justice.'"

8. Writing Properly

1. The Building Blocks of an Essay

I can comfortably say that poor writing is the most prevalent problem with low-graded essays. When grading papers, I spend around 75% of my time providing feedback on the student's writing. Effective writing is the flesh and blood of good essays. There is no such thing as a good essay that is poorly written. Using poor writing for your essay is like trying to build a house by haphazardly piling up bricks made of Jell-O and using cooking oil for cement: it's all going to end up a messy heap. The arguments will not come across clearly, the narrative will be muddled and hard to follow, and you will not be displaying strong knowledge and understanding. Most of all, it makes the work look ill-prepared, unprofessional, rushed and shoddy. It is not forgivable and will result in very weak grades.

Hopefully some of your tutors have been kind enough to start highlighting potential issues with your writing or common typos, mistakes or errors that might be creeping into your work, if there are any. If your tutors are not doing this, it does not always mean the errors are not there. Quite often, tutors do not have the time to address the minutiae of grammatical issues, typos, punctuation misuse and formatting errors. Certainly, some papers from particularly gifted students can display little to no writing issues, with only very infrequent and minor errors or typos. Many other papers, however, present a litany of writing errors, poor sentence structuring, grammatical failures, erratic punctuation and jarring typos. These papers will usually get very poor marks, even if the precise writing issues are not patiently pinpointed by the tutor.

Chapter 2 discussed just how crucial your written communication skills are when constructing an essay. Of course, certain disciplines may place *slightly* less emphasis on writing skills. An English, Law or Media tutor is likely to mark more strictly on writing quality than a tutor from a heavily numerical discipline, like Mathematics, Engineering or Economics. That said, there is no single discipline where poor written communication is excused when it comes to essays. Writing is the life force of essays. Of course, this can be especially challenging for students with certain writing disabilities or who are writing in a non-native language or who, quite simply, never had the fortune of good writing tuition in childhood. We tutors are alive to those challenges. However, we cannot excuse students from the same responsibilities to become excellent communicators that we expect from their peers. It just means that those students must work extra hard to improve, while taking all the additional support and adjustments they can.

Fortunately, writing is something that constantly improves and can be bettered and enhanced throughout your life. No learning on effective communication will ever go to waste. The best thing a student can do, therefore, is read the rest of this chapter. It explores lots of common writing issues in essays and provides troubleshooting advice and tips. Chapter 9 then continues the work on writing by looking at specific writing approaches, such as concise writing, reflective writing and writing in the correct perspective.

2. Becoming an Excellent Writer

As noted, the quality of your writing will continually improve the more you work on it and the more you practice. I have seen too many students who seem resigned to the idea they are never going to be gifted writers, so they just give up trying. Every day is an opportunity to improve, and these three steps are the key to your writing continually improving: (1) using all feedback; (2) conscious reading; and

(3) effective proofreading. All three of these steps are mutually reinforcing: the more you work on one, the more effective your work on the others will be.

1) Using All Feedback

Feedback is crucial to improving your writing. As noted, your tutors may not all be as thorough as me when it comes to correcting minor writing issues and errors. Any writing weaknesses they do highlight are likely to be those that are particularly significant or prevalent in your work. You should take notice of feedback like this. Make sure that you engage deeply with why the feedback was given and, as importantly, how you will fix this problem moving forward. This means using every opportunity to submit written work if you can, including engaging with formative assessments, so that your written work can receive maximum feedback. All feedback is golden when it comes to perfecting your essay writing craft.

It is not just feedback you might get from your submitted work which merits close attention. If you have any opportunity to have your work proofread and improved by a second pair of eyes, such as a family member or friend, then take it. Do not just accept their amendments; process and internalize them as well. For those who are really looking to succeed and who are determined to improve their essays, another good source feedback on your writing is using an expert proofreader. A good option for this is the huge range of high-quality academic proofreaders on **Fiverr**. Another alternative is to use my service, at AcademyWorks.co.

2) Conscious Reading

A large aspect of effective writing is effective reading. If a student has poor writing skills, it means that they are not absorbing the correct way of writing from everything they are reading. There is accurate writing around us all day, with plenty of opportunities to observe how sentences are structured, how punctuation is used and how to make writing clear and presentable. Start noticing this more. Look at how commas, colons, semicolons, periods, dashes, quotation marks and parentheses are all used. Look at the formulation of a complete sentence and how to order the words within that sentence to achieve different emphases. I call this conscious reading: not just reading the content, but being conscious of how that content is being presented and constructed.

It is important here to focus only on those materials that are *well written*. As such, posts and memes on social media, or the messages you receive from friends, are all out. I would say that 80-90% of the content on the internet is written atrociously. It is alarming how few people understand how to write these days. It seems like a self-perpetuating problem: because everyone writes poorly, others copy poor practice, only to normalize poor writing further. Unfortunately, when it comes to essay writing, this widespread type of informal writing will grade poorly. We are looking for proper, quality writing at university. To observe this, focus on high quality newspapers and magazines, non-fiction books published by reputable publishers or peer-reviewed academic journals. All these materials will pride themselves on writing accuracy and efficacy. The writing will also have been subject to rigorous proofreading and editing.

3) Effective Proofreading

It is hard to overstate the importance of effective *proofreading* when it comes to effective writing. By this, I mean reading through your work carefully, multiple times, to fix errors, improve the flow of the writing, try different sentence structures and to enhance the structure and layout. As has been noted, for most people, writing is a process of initially getting all the words down and then continually refining. This is a good writing technique, as it helps you to prevent brain block and just get all the thoughts, feelings and ideas out. Even if you are someone who tries to write every sentence perfectly first time, you will still need

8. Writing Properly

to have a rigorous process of checking, proofreading and perfecting at the end. No one writes anything perfectly first time—only by the fourth or fifth time!

It has happened too many times where a student has told me that they will make sure to leave plenty of time to proofread their next essay, only to hand in another substandard essay that looks rushed and messy. Then, when I ask what happened, they explain that they failed to leave enough time and rushed at the end. Let us start breaking this habit and ensuring that we work in at least an extra day, if not more, within our essay preparation timeline for rigorous proofreading, editing and perfecting. Also, work on improving your proofreading practice. Here are some tips:

✓ **Read at different paces**

Proofreading is about reading carefully to identify potential issues and errors (copy editing). It is also about checking the overall flow, pace and structure (structural editing). Both require different reading speeds and different focuses. For example, to identify potential errors, typos and punctuation misuse, you might need to read every sentence more slowly and carefully. To ensure that the writing has a good flow or reduce repetition, sometimes it helps to read it with more pace. Reading it at least more than once, once slowly and once slightly faster, should therefore help your proofreading.

✓ **Read at different times**

Our brain operates at different levels at different times of day. Also, the more we become immersed in a piece of work, the more we lose track of the bigger picture or become accustomed to its idiosyncrasies. It can therefore be quite effective to proofread at different times of the day or, at the very least, to take a good break before you begin a major final proofread. Some even suggest making sure you get a good night's sleep before embarking on the final editing and perfecting process.

✓ Check for multiples of the same error

If you might identify an error or weakness in your writing, consider whether the work might contain multiples of this error. For example, if you have misspelled a word and know that this word is likely to appear again, then conduct a search (Ctrl + F) to identify if that spelling mistake has occurred again elsewhere. It is not just spelling mistakes. You may spot certain formatting inconsistencies—be it line spacing, font sizes, subheadings, bullet points, and so on—that need to be checked throughout the document. It could be a misuse of punctuation, like a failure to insert a closed quotation bracket, which should then be checked document-wide.

✓ Enjoy the process

Okay, I know this sounds silly, but I mean it! Proofreading and perfecting should really be the most enjoyable aspect of your work and you should see it as such. You have done all the *hard* work: dedicated hours in the library, reading lots of material, trying different structures, hours of planning, pushing out every word and idea on the page, and so on. Proofreading's a satisfying process of rapidly converting charcoal into a beautiful diamond. With every tweak, fix and improvement, the work is exponentially lifted. Like when we were treasure hunting in the library in Chapter 3, we are treasure hunting here too—having fun hunting for fixes!

✓ Listen to the spellchecker

There are certain errors that creep into students' writing and you wonder how they missed it with today's word processors. Make sure that your word processing program (e.g., Word or Pages) has its spellchecker fully enabled, operating with the right language and correcting both spelling *and* grammar. When checking it is in the correct language, make sure that you are using the right dialect that you need (e.g., there is an important distinction between English (US), English (UK) and English (Australia), for example). 95% of the spelling errors picked up by your spellchecker will be actual spelling errors. Only things like names or rare words should be exceptions. The grammar corrections are more hit and miss, but they are significantly improving (maybe 80% accurate). Everything highlighted needs to be checked. All matters identified by the spellchecker should be closely considered and, unless confident, you should accept proposed corrections.

✓ **Print out your essay**

Reading your work in different mediums is great for many reasons. Mixing up your studying style to do some work off-screen might even help to improve concentration and your mental well-being. Moreover, reading a final draft of your work in printed form enables you to read it in a different light and with a different level of focus, helping you see issues more clearly. Seeing your work laid out on a sheet of paper can also make typos, errors and formatting issues more obvious to the eye. Enjoy the process of waking up in the morning and sitting with a coffee and a printout of your draft essay, while using a pen to note errors, typos and any issues with the writing.

✓ **Use 'Read Aloud' feature**

Similarly, it could help to change the medium from 'reading' to 'listening'. I find the automatic narration (or 'Read Aloud') feature in your word processor to be helpful for this. The computer will use your punctuation, syntax and structure to help determine the pace and flow of the narration. While it is not perfect, it might help identify areas where the delivery needs to slow down or speed up. Most helpfully, listening closely to your work being read aloud can help you identify errors and typos, given that they often stick out like a sore thumb on hearing them. But do not see Read Aloud as a substitute for separate visual proofreading. It will not accurately highlight grammatical or punctuation errors in you writing. Instead, see it as an additional bonus for checking the general flow and to detect glaring errors.

- ✓ **Always be proofreading**

The most important time to be proofreading and perfecting your work is undoubtedly at the end, when you have it all together as a coherent whole. Nevertheless, as noted in Chapter 4, proofreading and perfecting is an ongoing process that should be taking place at all times. Sometimes it is good to take a break from writing, especially if you are starting to stall, and instead to work back through your draft to perfect, tweak and tidy.

- ✓ **Use a second pair of eyes**

The importance of this was noted above, so I will not labour the point too much. However, there is frankly no substitute for having someone who is a skilled writer and communicator read through your work carefully to identify errors, formatting issues, structural weaknesses and areas where the writing could be better executed. It is not permissible to have your essay written by another person. Doing this has resulted in students being suspended or expelled, with a red flag against their name. It will certainly result in a Fail mark as well.

However, you are perfectly permitted to use another person to help you perfect *your* delivery and execution. Why is this permissible? Well, because it is realistic considering our working practices. I do not publish a paper without it being checked several times by colleagues. I do not write an exam question without it being checked by my peers. I have used an editor for this book. Using another person to iron out errors is a good thing. What would be wrong is if I claimed credit for that paper or exam question but did not write it!

2. Common Writing Problems

There is plenty that could be said on fixing common writing errors. However, I will pinpoint the most common errors that I see, as well as highlight some useful resources to support students across these areas. This will help you to identify

8. Writing Properly

where you could be going wrong and then help you to locate the relevant advice and support.

Informal Language

What you might realize from reading this book and throughout feedback from your work, is that academic writing has a particular style and tone compared to the types of writing you might be used to. Put simply, you cannot write using casual or informal language, hoping this will be sufficient to convey your evidence, ideas and analysis. Your writing needs to exude professionalism, objectivity and demonstrate complete literary competence. In many ways, you should imagine you are addressing a formal petition to the King of England, not a quick WhatsApp message to a friend!

Such professional academic writing carries a number of important implications. For example, its means ideas *expressed as* solely **personal opinions** have no place. Everything needs to be raised and critiqued in an *objective* manner and with a focus on evidence, rationality and analysis (see more in Chapter 3). This means you should *never* use phrases like, "I think", "I believe" or "In my opinion". In fact, as Chapter 9 explores, in many cases you should not write in the first person at all. Discussion should always be centred on an objective, rational and formal approach to critiquing evidence, ideas and materials. This makes the essay much more professional, persuasive and reliable.

Another implication of the need to write in formal essay language is that you must never use **contractions**, such as *don't, can't, isn't, won't, we've,* and so on. You need to write the full words, e.g., *do not, cannot, is not,* etc. (Of course, this book is not an academic essay, so *I'm* excused from the same rules on this one!) Apostrophes are therefore really the preserve of possessive pronouns (for example, if referring to Smith's article). Emojis are also out, of course! What is more, you must avoid **colloquialisms or slang**. In the UK, for example, informal slang such as saying, "She was taking the mickey" or "He was not her cup of tea", would have no place in an essay. The only exception might be where you were specifically using a well-known phrase or idea as a metaphor or illustration of a concept (e.g., arguing that a theory is *actually* "pear-shaped" or that an author's poetry evokes feelings of being "on thin ice").

Sentence Structuring

Perhaps the most common writing problem I see is sentence structuring and, particularly, the issues of sentence *fragments* and *run-on*. Sentence run-on is when a sentence has two or more independent clauses that are not split up into shorter sentences or which lack a conjunction. Look at the following example:

I feel very tired because it's been a long day, I think I should go to bed.

These are two independent clauses, but they are only separated by a comma. One way to split them up could be to introduce a conjunction, like "so" or "and". So, it would read like this:

I feel very tired because it's been a long day, so I think I should go to bed.

However, if we only ever do this we get to the common problem of *over-long* sentences. Not only are over-long sentences difficult to read and create muddled structure, but they invite grammatical errors and unsuccessfully connected clauses. They are also evidence of a lack of proofreading. I often remark to students that they should not be afraid of full stops! It is perfectly fine to end a sentence, input a period, and start a new sentence. Getting used to finishing a sentence and starting new ones is an incredibly important practice for students to work on. So, looking at our first example, a perhaps better way of writing it would probably be:

8. Writing Properly

I feel very tired because it's been a long day. I think I should go to bed.

This could be better because both are perfectly strong independent clauses, and they follow nicely on from each other. The meaning is just as clear, if not more. But, more importantly, it is much easier to read. This is a frequent issue for students. I have seen over-long sentences far too often. As an extreme, but entirely realistic, example:

Incorrect
There is something quite fun about writing without the use of full stops because it, sometimes, although rarely does, allow me to keep on talking despite the fact that the sentence should really be broken up and made into more manageable chunks that the reader can actually digest, because it's important to remember that a full stop represents an important pause or some kind of break and that the reader will never be able to keep up in and of course, however if broken into different sections and permutations, the sentence never ends which is fun for me, as a writer, because I can just waffle for ages and it will go on and on forever or until I decide to stop, start or stop again because it suits me perfectly well, and not the reader.

Correct
There is something quite fun about writing with the use of full stops. You can still keep talking, but your work will be broken up into more manageable chunks that your reader can actually digest. Indeed, full stops represent an important pause for the reader, allowing them to keep up. It also improves conciseness and prevents the work from waffling unnecessarily.

In general, you want to get a good mix of short and longer sentences in your work, as it will break the pace up nicely: shorter sentences can be quite punchy and quick, whereas longer sentences can convey a sense of being drawn-out and giving deeper detail. Practicing sentence structure is a long-term skill and even the most experienced writers will admit to a lack of technical knowledge about complex syntactical minutiae. Nevertheless, the general principle—as we all know—is that a complete sentence usually requires a *subject, object* and a *verb*. For example, "The dog is black" = The dog (subject) is (verb) black (object). The realities can be more complex than this. A common exception, for example, is when a sentence represents a reply or an order to do something, such as "Stop that!" or "No, thank you."

This brings us to another common sentence structuring error I see, being sentence *fragments*. These are incomplete sentences that do not successfully complete before a period is entered. In effect, they are the opposite problem of sentence run-on. I am often faced with the difficulty of having a student trying to adapt to my feedback suggesting they use shorter sentences, who then goes too far the other way and starts incorporating fragments! Seen from a technical perspective, therefore, fragments are sentences that are missing the key verb or object. For example:

Incorrect
The new accord developed by the United States and adopted by many other states.

Incorrect
The new accord developed by the United States and adopted by many other states has achieved.

Correct
The new accord developed by the United States and adopted by many other states has achieved this.

In the first sentence you can see that we just have the subject (the new accord), but no object or verb. The second sentence includes a verb ("has achieved"), but still has no object ("this"). Another common cause of fragments is when a transitional phrase is used (see Chapter 6), but it is not completed. For example:

Incorrect

However, the last participant, who was looking unhappy with the situation.
That said, there is something that.

The transitional phrases ("However" and "That said") in fact have little effect here. The cause of the fragment is the lack of verb and subject: we have an unhappy participant, but they are not described as anything or as doing something. Nevertheless, students often miss the completion of a sentence following a transition phrase because the sentence is longer and easier to lose track of.

Another common cause of sentence fragments is an incomplete **verb phrase**. This is tricker to spot because it looks like the sentence has an object, subject and verb. Nevertheless, because of the way the verb phrase (verb + subject) is written, it has opened up a new phrase that needs to be completed. For example:

Incorrect

I told my dog to stop chasing its.
There is no reason that he should ever need to do.

Similarly, we have the issue of **dependent clauses**. These cannot be sentences in themselves, as they are dependent on another clause. Without the other clause, they become meaningless.

After I have finished.
When the clock strikes midnight.

The point is to always be aware of sentence structure. If sentences are getting too long, practice tightening them. This will help your sentences to make more direct and clear points. I often inform students that they should use "punchier and more direct" sentences. In other words, try have one clear *singular* point that each sentence is trying to make. If your sentence is trying to cover too much or has multiple points, it is very likely too long. In such cases, you should either break the sentence up into multiple sentences or, if it does not look too clunky and you understand their meaning, use punctuation such as colons, dashes or semicolons to allow for more points to be smoothly incorporated. Most importantly, keep practising and observing proper sentence structure around you.

Grammar and Syntax

Although sentence run on and fragments are perhaps the most common grammatical weakness I see, there are a huge range of other common culprits. I have compiled a list of ones that I have seen far more frequently in student essays than you might imagine. It is also worth noting that I see these weaknesses in native speakers just as much, if not more, than students for whom English is a second language. I therefore urge all essay writers not to assume they are already expert.

Auxiliary verbs provide a tense or extended meaning to pronouns like *she, he, it, we, everyone* and *they.* For example, "He *has* nearly finished." This is often called a conjugation, where a verb is used to reflect certain characteristics. However, it is extremely common for auxiliary verbs—including words such as *can / could, do / does* and *have / has*—to get mixed up.

8. Writing Properly

For example:
She have a black cat = She has a black cat
The cat was coming tomorrow and I am excited = The cat is coming tomorrow and I am excited
That cat do run fast = That cat does run fast
There is other cats here for her to play with = There are other cats here for her to play with
What is you? = What are you?

Relatedly, it is common to see **verb tenses** generally mixed up. In many ways, verb tenses are about describing *actions* in the past, present and future. I include a very useful example from Walden University below. Although it is an extreme example, it does illustrate the different tenses perfectly:

- Simple present: *She **writes** every day.*
- Present progressive: *She **is writing** right now.*
- Simple past: *She **wrote** last night.*
- Past progressive: *She **was writing** when he called.*
- Simple future: *She **will write** tomorrow.*
- Future progressive: *She **will be writing** when you arrive.*
- Present perfect: *She **has written** Chapter 1.*
- Present perfect progressive: *She **has been writing** for 2 hours.*
- Past perfect: *She **had written** Chapter 3 before she started Chapter 4.*
- Past perfect progressive: *She **had been writing** for 2 hours before her friends arrived.*
- Future perfect: *She **will have written** Chapter 4 before she writes Chapter 5.*
- Future perfect progressive: *She **will have been writing** for 2 hours by the time her friends come over.*

Verbs can sometimes stay the same across certain tenses, but the auxiliary verb (conjugation) changes. For example, "She **is** studying", "She **was** studying" or "She **will be** studying." Other times the verb also must change tense. For example, "She **has studied**" or "She **will study**." It is important to continually develop awareness of how verb and conjugations move around and change depending on the tense. Sometimes errors creep in, even when you know the correct way to write it. It is therefore good to weed out such errors when proofreading, as well as to continually develop awareness of your own frequent errors.

Another quite common problem for those with weaker English skills is applying the **wrong pronoun** (e.g., his, her, my, our, their, its, everyone, none, no one) to a noun. This is far more common than you might imagine, and you likely do it yourself from time to time.

Some examples:
Everyone is doing his best = Everyone is doing their best
I have forgotten each one's name = I have forgotten everyone's name
John lost its keys = John lost his keys

Related to this problem is that of **ambiguous pronouns**. This is where a sentence has a pronoun linked to two nouns, but it is not clear which noun the pronoun is referring to. For example, "Shelter does a lot of brilliant work in poorer London boroughs, where they always need help." Is it Shelter who always need the help or the London boroughs? Technically, given that organizations—such as Shelter—are grammatically treated as single units, rather than a collective ("it", rather than "they"), we might guess that it is referring to the London boroughs. But it is certainly not clear. Another example might be: "Janie met with Jenny because she needed to talk." Which one needed to talk? Think about your choice of words in such instances to prevent ambiguity and uncertainty.

8. Writing Properly

In terms of sentence structure, **adverbs** should usually come immediately before the verb to which they are applied or at the end of the sentence. Adverbs can be thought of as words describing a verb and are commonly based on adjectives ending with 'ly'. Examples include *quickly, happily, amazingly, usually, commonly, dramatically, unbelievably, coolly, sneakily,* and so on. The point is to think carefully about where the adverb goes in the sentence, to ensure that it is sufficiently attached to the verb or has the right tense. Examples of adverbs being in the wrong place include:

*The man slowly was speaking = The man was speaking **slowly***
*You speak well English = You speak English **well***
*The green hurriedly lizard skittered along the floor = The green lizard skittered along the floor **hurriedly** / The green lizard skittered **hurriedly** along the floor*

Or, if an adverb is applied to an adjective, it should be immediately before the adjective phrase. For example:
*They are **unbelievably** strong.*
*That is **quite** difficult.*

Another good practice is to avoid **double negatives**. Although they can be technically correct grammatically speaking, they are prone to error and are difficult to read.
She is never not here = She is always here / Rarely is she not here.
He won't stop stopping = He keeps stopping.

Use **or** with **either** or **nor** with **neither**.
***Either** I'll lose and will be gutted; **or** I'll win and will be ecstatic!*
*It's **either** blue **or** red.*
*It's **neither** blue **nor** red.*
*I am **neither** happy **nor** sad.*

In fact, either-or and neither-nor are just examples of **prepositional idioms**, which are another very common area of confusion. There are a huge number of phrases that require specific prepositions to achieve the correct meaning or where the wrong preposition will generate the wrong meaning. Here are just some examples where the prepositions needed for the phrase are quite specific or where the wrong preposition creates the wrong phrase:

- *I am keen to* **participate with** *this competition* = *I am keen to* **participate in** *this competition*
- *I did it on the* **back off** *several defeats* = *I did it on the* **back of** *several defeats*
- *It was hard to* **agree by** *each other* = *It was hard to* **agree with** *each other*
- *He* **backed up** *because he was anxious* = *He* **backed out** *because he was anxious*
- *He* **passed out** *the opportunity* = *He* **passed up** *the opportunity*

Further common issues include a switching of verb tenses:

- *The experiment* **became** *challenging because it* **involves** *human participants* = *it involved.*
- *Pittman et al* **propose** *that* **future** *experiments should* **have included** *a control* = *should include.*

Another is the incorrect application between adverbs and adjectives:

- *There is still a strong demand for* **essentially** *goods* = *essential goods.*
- *Quite* **alarming,** *the study suggests that most species have less than a century left* = *quite alarmingly.*

Another is the incorrect application between plurals and singulars:

- *All the cats in the picture* **has** *three legs* = *have.*
- *Pittman et al* **argues** = *argue.*
- *Quite alarmingly, the study* **suggest** *that most species have less than a century left* = *suggests.*

Finally, a further common grammatical error is getting the **wrong indefinite article** (*a* vs. *an*) before a noun. The article "a" should be used with words starting with a consonant sound and "an" should be used with words starting with a vowel sound (that is *a, e, i, o, u*). For example, *a dog, a cat, an umbrella,* an *outstanding achievement*. Of course, a tricky issue is that certain words might start with a consonant, but still have a vowel *sound,* so are still preceded by *an*. For example, "It's in half an *hour*" or "It's been an *honour,* madam". Or they may start with a vowel but have a consonant sound. For example, "It is a United Nations agreement." This can be particularly tricky with acronyms, as it is based on whether they are pronounced as their component letters (e.g., PhD, MBA, FYI, APA, UFO) or as their own word (e.g., PEAL, SWOT, NASA, UNESCO, KISS). So, for example, one would usually write "a UFO" and "an MBA".

Punctuation

Another extremely common weakness in student writing is the ritual misuse and misunderstanding of punctuation. Punctuation is such an essential tool and critical aspect of writing. Without it, entire meanings of text can be lost or made unclear. Proper punctuation not only looks professional, but it improves the readability, flow and structure of your entire narrative. It is important to remember that the tutors grading your work will be trying to read it as rapidly as possible. If you are using poor punctuation that makes it difficult to follow on the first read, the tutor is unlikely to go back and read it again. More likely they will try to continue in a more confused state, before criticizing the muddled and vague writing in their feedback. Make the job of interpreting your work easy by getting all your punctuation right—or as right as possible!

I am confident in most students' abilities to understand the **full stop** or **period** (.). I think most students know how a full stop or period works—or at least should work. There is a question around whether acronyms should have periods between letters, which is discussed in Chapter 9. Otherwise, my concern is more with students understanding when a sentence should end and a new one should begin, as discussed above. Instead of continually linking everything up with commas, semicolons, hyphens or God forbid, an ellipsis (…), please try to be more assertive at ending sentences properly with a period and starting new ones.

Perhaps the most misused form of punctuation is the **comma**. This is in some ways understandable, given that the rules around them are complex and not always black-and-white. However, it is really important—taking into account the advice above to continually advance your writing proficiency and to observe effective writing around you more closely—that you work hard to perfect the comma as much as possible. The four ways that a comma is most frequently used can be quite easily explained:

- Between two *dependent* clauses in the sentence. For example:
  If it does not arrive soon, I am going to have a meltdown.
  It depends on what time it is, as well as who's coming.

- To separate items in a list. For example:
  For breakfast we ate eggs, bacon, mushrooms and beans.
  The lake was huge, cold and dark.

- After certain conjunctions or transition phrases. For example:
  However, it has not always been the case.
  Nevertheless, it could well work.

- To provide additional information given in the middle of a sentence. This often known as a non-defining clause, as it is not an essential aspect of the sentence's subject-verb-object. It is usually done by sandwiching the information between two commas. For example:
  Mr Rogers, the burly taxman, was at the door.

8. Writing Properly

The weather, which would not stop changing, was jeopardizing the experiment.

A remarkable number of students also get mixed up in their use of **apostrophes**. There are two main areas where apostrophes appear: contractions and possessives. Given that contracted words—such as *it's, cannot, won't, shouldn't, they've, we've,* and so on—should never appear in academic writing (see above), that only really leaves possessives.

Possessive apostrophes are when you indicate that something belongs to someone or something. For example, "That is the dog's breakfast" or "That jumper is Ross's." In an essay, these are likely to be quite rare, but they do still come up. It is important to recognize that if it is indicating possession by more than one of the thing, then the apostrophe comes after the *s*. For example, "That's the girls' favourite" would mean that it's a favourite of the multiple of girls (being a group of two or more). If the word indicates a plural already, then you could not have possession by more than one. For example, "That's everyone's favourite" or "It's the people's choice" would both be correct. Finally, one debate about possessive apostrophes is whether, with words ending in s, you should put s's or just s'. For example, should it be Jesus' or Jesus's? I think *Jesus's* is historically accurate, but either is fine. Just be consistent.

Apostrophes may also be placed between the *s* and the word when writing a plural of letters, numbers or when referring to multiples of a *word*. For example, 7's and *p*'s could be correct, as would be, "Count how many *charming*'s there are in your essay." But you do not use apostrophes for multiples of acronyms or time periods. For example, 1990's would be incorrect in British English (it would be 1990s), although it is correct in US English. Similarly, SME's would be incorrect if referring to multiple SMEs.

Unless specifically instructed, it is generally acceptable to adopt either single (' ') or double (" ") **quotation marks** when directly quoting others. Your discipline or course may give you clear guidance on which you should use, so follow this. The main thing, as always, is to be consistent. There is one extremely common problem I see a lot with quotation marks, which is the failure to close them. The same occurs with **brackets** ([ ]) and **parentheses** (( )). Square brackets are used to insert text, captions or comments into direct quotes. They indicate that the included components do not form part of the original quote. Parentheses are sometimes used in the main body to enclose incidental or supplemental information or comments. They can be extremely useful because the reader will read them like a side-comment, which does not distract away from the main thrust and pace of the story. When reading them you almost change volume, pace and tone, recognizing their separation from the main narrative. Start observing how they might be used occasionally in high quality academic writing.

Please make sure that all parentheses, brackets and quotation marks are successfully completed in pairs. This can take a bit of focus when you have got a complex sentence, such as those consisting of quotes within quotes or parentheses within parentheses. Just count them up and make sure that they fully complete as a pair and close. An extreme example with parentheses:

> (According to Shimwell, 'this ground-breaking event inspired to the heart-happy movement' (2003, 5-6) (although it seems likely this was before the break-free movement (Rose 2006)).)

Parentheses and brackets also fully enclose sentences. This means that the full stop after a sentence contained in brackets should be inside the brackets, as otherwise the full stop would be floating with nothing it is connected to. For example:

8. Writing Properly

Incorrect

It was submitted at 6pm. (This was the latest by which it could be submitted).

Correct

It was submitted at 6pm. (This was the latest by which it could be submitted.)

It is also worth students practising the use and application of **colons** (:) and **semicolons** (;). They can both be used to conjoin two independent clauses: in effect, two complete sentences. However, *only colons* can be used between a complete sentence and a fragment (as was done with the previous sentence). In other words, only colons can link a complete sentence (subject-verb-object) to a statement that is not a complete sentence: like this.

The choice between a colon and semicolon can get a little tricky and most English speakers will admit to being uncertain on the specific differences. In general, when linking two independent clauses, the colon is used when *clarifying* or *explaining* the first clause. The semicolon is used when flowing on from the first sentence, but not providing a specific *explanation* of that first sentence. The distinction is so subtle that it is sometimes hard to truly appreciate. For example, compare:

It was the most beautiful artwork: it was so pristine and perfect.
It was the most beautiful artwork; it could easily be worth a small fortune.

The first one (using the colon) is *explaining* the statement in the first clause. The second example (using the semicolon) is *not explaining* the first clause but just building on it.

Semicolons are also more suitable when a coordinating conjunction (e.g., *but, therefore, whereas, however*) is missing between the two sentences. For example,

'The dogs were loud; the cats were quiet.' This could have been separated with a comma followed by a word like 'but' or 'whereas', but a semicolon can work nicely for pairing the sentences together. Relatedly, semicolons are appropriate when the second sentence starts with a transitional phrase (e.g., *therefore, thus, nevertheless, but, for example*—see Chapter 6 for many more). Here you could also use a comma or input two sentences, as discussed above, but a semicolon might be used to show a strong *connection* between the clauses. For example, 'I misread the instructions; and, *consequently*, I failed to pass' or 'We couldn't stay awake anymore; we *therefore* had to stop.'

Finally, it was mentioned above that only colons can be used between a complete sentence and a fragment. This is usually to provide some kind of emphasis or conclusion to that first sentence: like this. As another example, "The day started off pretty much the same as every other day that week: cold and lonely." Colons are also used to begin a list. For example, "John had three majors: art, history and economics." Semicolons are used to generate long lists where commas are found within the items, acting as a bit of a super-comma. For example, "For breakfast we ate eggs, bacon and sausages; lunch was soup and toast; and dinner was lamb, peas and carrots."

To summarise, either a colon or semicolon can be used between two independent clauses (complete sentences). A writer also has the freedom to split these it into two sentences or to add a comma with a coordinating conjunction. The more you read and practice your understanding of punctuation, the more you will get a sense of which approaches are likely to work better. Certainly, do not over-use colons or semicolons. They are good to throw in occasionally, as they help break the pace up; but too many will make the writing messy and might only increase the chances of making an error.

8. Writing Properly

Similarly requiring years of practice for any good writer is the distinction between **hyphens** (-), **en dashes** (–) and **em dashes** (—). In a nutshell, the narrower hyphen is used to conjoin two words, like check-in, run-on, brother-in-law. The mid-sized en dash is used to connect two number or data points, like 7–8, 40–15, the London–Birmingham train. The longer em dash is a little bit more flexible. A common use is to use them in pairs within sentences as an alternative to parentheses ( ). They are a bit more pronounced than parentheses, so it will place greater emphasis and power on the enclosed information. For example, consider the sentence, "If it was not for his most famous discovery (being the existence of oxygen), things would be different today." In many ways, parentheses are not as effective here, because the information within the brackets is actually very important to the meaning of the sentence. It is not an extraneous sidenote, but an important caption within the sentence's meaning. Better, therefore, might be, "If it was not for his most famous discovery—the existence of oxygen—things would be different today."

I will sometimes use a pair of em dashes in a sentence like this, when I have to write a sentence with 3 or more different clauses—or, in other words, a very long sentence—which benefits from the division. Finally, an em dash can be used in place of colons or parentheses are the end of sentence when providing an additional thought, note or conclusion on the previous sentence. Take my example of a colon doing this above, "The day started off pretty much the same as every other day that week: cold and lonely." This could equally be, "The day started off pretty much the same as every other day that week—cold and lonely."

Finally, I am detecting a growing misunderstanding and misuse of **ellipses** (…). A lot of this is, again, caused by people observing poor practice on social media and thinking this is how you write properly. A particularly common misunderstanding is to think that ellipses can have variable lengths. I have seen too many passages of writing with ellipses of two or four or five dots all emerging,

like this: 'I cannot wait for the match this weekend.. It's gonna be a cracker......
we have even got our shirts....all ironed.. and ready to go......'. That is just wrong
in so many ways. Ellipses should *only* have 3 dots. You may rarely have a situation
where an ellipsis is omitting text within a quote, just before the sentence ends. In
such a case, the ellipsis (…) would be followed by a period (.), so it appears like
4 dots. For example:

*According to Smith, there are "many disadvantages to adopting this treatment
…. Their antimicrobial resistance makes them an especially unsuitable option for
immunocompromised patients" (2023, 5–6).*

This is really the only use of ellipses in academic writing: the omission of text in
a quote. It can be useful for removing wasted or superfluous words within a quote.
As discussed further in Chapter 9, it is important to reduce your reliance on direct
quotes and to paraphrase concepts as much as possible. If you are direct quoting,
you also want to chop it up or keep it as concise as possible.

The only other use for ellipses is to show hesitation or a trailing off thought when
writing someone's thoughts or speech. For example, 'It was on Saturday… err,
no wait… yeah, it was Saturday." You are never going to be writing from the
perspective of a character's inner thoughts or speech in an essay, so this should
never come up! One rare exception might be if you have conducted a study that
includes interviews and you are directly quoting things said by participants. This
might include hesitation.

Capitalization

Another extremely common problem I see is inaccurate or inconsistent
capitalization of words. Most students know that a capital letter should be used
at the start of a sentence. The more confusing issue appears to be the
capitalization of random words or confusion over proper nouns, i.e., names and

titles. Quite simply, if it is a name or title, it should be in title case (first letters capitalized). This means the name of people, departments or organizations are proper nouns that need capitalizing for every word. The same applies for titles, such as the name of a movie, book, article or official position or salutation (e.g., Sir, President, Senior Consultant, Senator, or Minister of Health). The titles of works, such as articles, books and movies, may also be italicized. It is important to also note that titles and salutations, as well as your essay's own subheadings and titles, should always be in **title case**. This means that preposition words like *of, the, in, and, at, by* and *to* are not capitalized (unless they are at the start of the sentence, of course).

Wrong	**Correct**
president of The United states	President of the United States
… The Secretary of state For health and Welfare	… the Secretary of State for Health and Welfare
Colombia, finland and iraq	Colombia, Finland and Iraq
Jonny williams	Jonny Williams
I've got my Final assessment tomorrow	I've got my final assessment tomorrow
The movie the perks of being a Wallflower	The movie *The Perks of Being a Wallflower*
It depends on which Parliament	It depends on which parliament
That is governed by westminster parliament	That is governed by Westminster Parliament
It is a matter for Government	It is a matter for government

| This site is monitored by HM government | This site is monitored by HM Government |

Notice the tricky words of parliament and government at the end. These are standard nouns that are not capitalized unless they are part of a title or name, such as Westminster Parliament or HM Government.

Spelling and Typos

It is hard to identify and diagnose all spelling errors and typos, as they are so diverse and random. As highlighted in the first section above, you should make full use of the spellchecker on your word processor. This will identify many spelling errors and either automatically correct them or underline them for your review. Of course, spellcheckers can sometimes flag something that is perfectly okay, such as an unusual name. They can also miss typos if the word is spelled incorrectly but is still the right kind of word (such as a noun or verb). For example, if you meant to write "We found the jacket on the dog", but instead wrote, "We found the jacket on the dig", then spellchecker will not notice because they are both nouns!

Another important practice when trying to eliminate spelling mistakes and typos is to make a note of your own common errors. Just for example, if you know that you sometimes get *to* and *too* mixed up, or *allowed* and *aloud*, or *they are*, *their* and *there*, then check for these issues specifically when you are proofreading. Such errors are common with **homophones**, which are words that sound the same but are spelt differently. Common examples include:

- *they are / their / there*
- *you are / your*
- *to / too / two*
- *bear / bare*

8. Writing Properly

- *it's / its*
- *here / hear*
- *who's / whose*
- *break / brake*
- *affect / effect*
- *flower / flour*
- *our / hour*
- *tire / tyre*

A very common area of confusion among these is the distinction between *its* and *it's*. Quite simply, the apostrophe is only used when it's a contraction of "it is". When we are using "its" as a possessive, such as "The photograph lost *its* sheen", then there is no apostrophe. Fortunately, to make things easy, in essays you should **never use contracted words!** It was discussed above that you should never use words like *it's, I'm, they're, would've, they've, you'd, can't* and *don't*. You must write the full words out. As such, the only "its" you should have will be the possessive kind, with no apostrophe.

Make sure to always **spell out acronyms on their first use.** For example, if you refer to the Human Rights Act as "HRA" or the United Nations Educational, Scientific and Cultural Organization as "UNESCO" in your essay, that is fine. However, make sure that the *first time* you write them you put, "Human Rights Act (HRA)" or "United Nations Educational, Scientific and Cultural Organization (UNESCO)". The acronym in the parentheses tells the reader that all references to HRA or UNESCO hereafter refer to this set of words.

While you want to be careful of overusing acronyms, they can be really useful for promoting concise language and saving words if you are frequently referring to the same concepts or ideas as part of your analysis. For example, if your essay is contrasting multilingual language processing with bilingual language processing, instead of writing them out every time, you might early on refer to "Multilingual Language Processing (MLP)" and to "Bilingual Language Processing (BLP)". Then you could just refer to MLP and BLP throughout your paper: which is much better!

Other than this, there is not a lot more that can be done to eliminate typos and spelling mistakes other than being thorough and effective in your proofreading and continuing to develop your writing skills and practices. A good option is to use **Grammarly.com**, which is a sophisticated proofreading and grammar-checking service which, for millions of people, has now become indispensable. Another guaranteed method of being effective in your proofreading is, of course, using an expert essay editor to look through your work and make the necessary adjustments. One option here is to use my services, available at **AcademyWorks.co** or to choose from a huge range of experts on **Fiverr.com**.

9. Writing Approaches

1. Writing in the First and Third Person

An important essay approach you might have to adopt is writing in the "third" or "first" person. Certainly, in the humanities disciplines, where third person is standard, students can find this style tricky to adapt to. This chapter first distinguishes between these two essay styles and their key differences, before giving some tips and hints on ensuring you stay in the right perspective in your assignment.

Writing in the **first person** means you would be writing your paper from *your* perspective. You would therefore say things like:
"In this paper, *I* argue that..."
"*We* tested this hypothesis against the research data and found..."
"*I* would surmise that..."

This is increasingly common in science-based disciplines, including the social sciences, which are built on the foundations of practical and empirical research. By contrast, the **third person** is more common in the humanities and arts, as well as law and business disciplines. Here, by contrast, there must be *no* first person or reference to oneself. Everything should be written from an objective/neutral standpoint, looking at it from an apathetic vantage point. The above might therefore become:
"This paper argues that..."
"Testing this hypothesis against the research data, it can be seen that..."
"It could be surmised that..."

In some assessments you may be asked to adopt the first person for that specific assessment only. Common examples might be where you are asked to engage in writing a reflective essay or to undertake an exercise like writing a letter. Similarly, look out for instructions if you are in a scientific discipline, as some assignments may require an objective third person approach too. However, unless instructed otherwise, you should adopt whatever style is the standard for your discipline.

Why the Distinction?

It is very important to get the distinction between these two approaches and to ensure you adopt the right one for your academic work. In truth, it is perhaps less of a concern if a scientist strays into the third person, as their analysis and arguments can still be driven by the data and the research findings. That said, being in the first person perhaps allows a scientist to connect with their audience and to align their personal insights with their research.

It is perhaps more of a concern when a student from a humanities-style discipline ventures into writing in the first person. In such cases you are likely to get red pen through it and to lose marks. These disciplines emphasize the development of argument through an objective analysis of evidence. You are thus seeking to develop a rational and neutral evaluation among the data and existing materials, working from an outwardly emotionless standpoint. Venturing into the first person makes your work appear instead based on *opinion*, rather than rational deduction. It also risks making the work appear more like a campaign piece, rather than an academic essay.

A pet hate of tutors who work in third person disciplines, such as law, history, languages, business and the arts, is when students make clear that something is purely opinion. We detest seeing words like "In my opinion", "I believe" or "I think". Some tutors even write in big red marker, in response, "I DO NOT CARE WHAT YOUR OPINION IS". I am not that cruel, although I do share the frustration. The point is that you are trying to persuade the reader based on objective and rational analysis of evidence; and the third person is considered more objective and rational in tone.

First Person Writing

Writing in the first person is perhaps a more natural process for many. It is quite easy first-person disciplines to use both first and third person perspectives in a piece, with it remaining appropriate in style and tone. There are two critically important requirements though. First, simply, make sure to only use "we" or "us" in the context of the authors (you) if there is more than one author of the paper or it is made clear that more than one person was involved in conducting the research (i.e., it refers to work you did in a group). Do not say "We suggest that" or "To us it appeared", when just one person conducted the research and wrote the paper. The same goes for using "we" when referring to society in general or when including the reader of the paper: both can be problematic. For example, avoid saying things like, "We all know that climate change is accelerating rapidly" or "We are next going to examine the issues presented by Smith." They seem to treat the reader as if they a co-collaborator, but they are just a spectator.

More importantly, even though they write in the first person, scientific disciplines are still built on the foundations of objective and rational analysis of evidence. As such, you still need to avoid writing in a subjective style, saying things such as "I believe that…" or "In my opinion…". Adopt a more objective and rational tone, even if from your *own* perspective. When discussing evidence or engaging in analysis, you might therefore be better served by moving into a third person perspective ("The evidence suggests that…" or "According to the data…"). When discussing what you actually *did*, you can write in the first person ("We conducted a contextual analysis…" or "I then interviewed the test subjects under laboratory conditions…"). If referring to something that could be an opinion of the authors, qualify the language and tone (e.g., "We could hypothesize that..." or "It is proposed that...").

Third Person Writing

Students often find transitioning into writing in the third person a little unusual at first. They can particularly find it difficult to develop arguments or indicate their perspective without saying "I", "my" and "me", or without referring to "the author". Some students also have an impression that writing in the third person prevents them from developing their own opinions or perspectives, which is not the case. You can very much have an opinion and be developing an interesting or engaging argument, all with the use of an objective third person tone. It is simply about steering the reader to draw those same conclusions from the evidence and the arguments proffered. Through your shaping of the discussion and the prominence you give to different ideas and hypotheses, you can certainly get your own ideas and perspectives across.

Writing well in the third person is really about practice. It is also about reading purposefully in your discipline and getting more familiar with the tones, styles and practices of the scholars in your field. The key is simply to use alternative connecting phrases. Some examples include:
"It can be deduced that…"
"It appears from this analysis that…"
"One might question this, because…"
"From the evidence, it is possible to hypothesize…"
"It is clear that…"
"Although this appears persuasive, there are critical issues that remain."
"One particular issue is that…"
"According to Meyer and Brudwick (2016), this is unlikely because…"
"Whether or not this is accurate depends on a number of factors…"
… and so on.

Finally, although referring to "the author" is technically in the third person (e.g., "The author would argue that…" or "In the author's opinion…"), it is still regarded as bad practice and just another way of writing in the first person. Similarly, students writing in the third person sometimes resort to referring to "one", known as an impersonal pronoun, to avoid referring to themselves. For example, "One could argue that…" or "One might be of the opinion that…". In general, this is okay if the language is qualified ("one might" or "one could", as opposed to "one would" or "one should"). Indeed, it remains in the third person and remains objective in tone. However, try not to over-use it and instead practice other neutral stylistic approaches, like those above.

A Final Point on Plural Pronouns

It was noted above that first person authors should perhaps only refer to "we" if there are clearly two or more people involved in the research. For writers in both first and third person, however, authors need to be careful using plural pronouns when referring to other contexts. Some examples of incorrect use of plural pronouns:

"Our government has not developed regulations to address this."
"Brexit was bad for us politically and economically."
"We Americans tend to value liberty above all else…"
"As feminists, we are aware of the inequalities."
"China has a different model of corporate governance, where they…"

In these cases, the use of a plural pronoun works to identify the author(s) as belonging to one group and distinguishing them from other groups. It creates an "us" and "them" theme, which is inappropriate for most academic writing. Again, academics want to remain married to evidence, data and rationality throughout, and thereby avoid coming across as operating from any one perspective or developing arguments based on personal views or backgrounds. It is better to write these things in an objective, neutral tone, where the writer appears apathetic and omnipresent. For example:

"The UK government has yet to develop regulations to address this."

"Brexit has been regarded as politically and economically harmful to the United Kingdom."

"American culture is well-known for placing significant value on personal liberties."

"Feminist scholars are aware of the inequalities presented."

"China adopts a different model of corporate governance, which…".

Two final notes about perspectives in writing. Make sure that you also use **non-gendered language** wherever possible. Your tutors will be concerned and mindful of all matters relating to equality, equal opportunity and bias. A very common issue I see, for example, is students referring to company directors or doctors as "he", or assuming that a board's chairperson is a "chairman". By the same token, and just as problematically, I have seen nurses and air stewards assumed to be a "she". Simply use pronouns such as "they" or titles like "chairperson" to ensure broader representation. Finally, **avoid referring to the reader as "you"**, unless specifically instructed otherwise. It can sound a little patronizing or accusatory. For example, you would not say something like, "However, you need to consider the alternatives in this scenario."

2. Concise Writing

Writing concisely—that is conveying information clearly with fewer words—is a truly essential skill when it comes to assignments and coursework. It is hard to overstate just how important it is. One of the most significant advantages of writing concisely is that you can free up space in your essay for the richer and more analytical discussions to secure you that stronger grade. Crucially, it also significantly improves the quality, readability, flow and power of your writing. It is a core aspect of effective essay structure and presentation.

9. Writing Approaches

This section introduces 13 ideas for how to make your writing more concise and to make your essays thereby more powerful and engaging. To begin, I should just say that I am not a *naturally* concise writer. Most people aren't. It takes practice and perseverance. However, the more you become aware of the skills and practices of concise writing, the more instinctive and ritualized it becomes. I therefore adopt the following steps to help me.

1) Remove Redundant and Unnecessary Phrases

The Merriam-Webster Dictionary defines *concise* as being "free from superfluous detail". Similarly, many explanations will direct focus towards the eradication of *redundancies*. This is a critical aspect of concise writing. It is a recognition that we can often say things far more clearly with far fewer words. One of the first culprits, therefore, is the use of **unnecessary qualifiers,** including words such as: *actually, really, basically, probably, very, definitely, somewhat, kind of, extremely, practically*. These should only be used when necessary to convey a very specific meaning: otherwise, leave them out. An example might be:

Incorrect

There are basically two points that definitely support this extremely interesting conclusion. These points practically form an argument absolutely against wholeheartedly adopting Taylorism somewhat.

Correct

There are two points that support this conclusion and that form an argument against adopting Taylorism.

This also relates to the need to avoid clunky sentences riddled with unnecessary words. This could mean amending phrases that require prepositional words, such as *for, in, on, at, over* and *through*. An example might be:

Incorrect
For the reasons stated already when discussing it just now, in thinking this way it is more likely that players are more likely to be victorious over their opponents if they climbed on the ladder.

Correct
It therefore appears likely that players will win if they climb the ladder.

Another common area where you can find redundant words is when using common sayings or turns of phrase. I personally use these a lot in emails to colleagues, but I would avoid them in academic writing. What is more, they are often idiomatic and do not always translate well for non-native speakers. For example:

Incorrect
When the chips are down and a team is close to throwing in the towel, it is time for all hands to be on deck and to the pump going ten to the dozen. Indeed, many hands make light work.

Correct
An effective team will work together when facing challenges.

It can also help if you avoid making overstatements or using superlative language. Just focus on being clear in meaning and direct, instead of resorting to emotive or overly expressive language. For example:

Incorrect
It is quite unbelievable and truly remarkable for one to ponder in amazement at the fact that all grass-eating species are ruminant.

Correct
It is noteworthy that all grass-eating species are ruminant.

2) Avoid Needless Repetition
You may be using two or three words where just one would suffice. This is particularly common when a word ultimately repeats the meaning of another word or adds little to it. For example:

Incorrect
Given the threatening risk of a changing transformation in the studied specimen, all allocated work had to be finally completed by later that day.

Correct
Given the risk of transformation in the specimen, all work had to be completed that day.

In effect, you want to remove unnecessary modifiers and unnecessary adjectives. The question should always be whether you can convey the same meaning in fewer words. If so, then it is likely better without the unnecessary words. Writers.com lists some common examples, such as:
  A period of 6 years = 6 years
  In my honest opinion, I think that = I think
  One and the same = The same
  A total of 25 carrots = 25 carrots
  Close proximity = Proximity
  Free gift = Gift
  In the event that = If

3) Avoid Multiple Adjectives or Nouns Where Possible

In a similar way, you want to avoid multiple adjectives or multiple nouns unless necessary to convey specific meaning. Adjectives are describing words. They are very common in flowery and colourful writing, such as in novels, but might play less of a role in an academic paper. By contrast, academic papers put greater emphasis on specifics, such as arguments, data, figures, statistics and facts.

Incorrect

The subject was wearing a soft, warm, fuzzy jumper with a small, bright, multicoloured LED light on the heart region, intended to alert the listening, attentive and engaged audience of his changing deep and heartfelt emotions.

Correct

The subject wore a multicoloured light on his heart that alerted the audience of his changing emotions.

The same can be said for multiple nouns that contribute little more collectively than one of the nouns alone. An example is:

Incorrect

She is a student studying the subject areas of business and history.

Correct

She is studying business and history.

A further way of thinking about this is to consider redundant pairs of words, such as *full and complete, each and every, hopes and dreams, whole entire, first and foremost, true and accurate, always and forever*. None of these phrases need three words and could use just one!

4) Eliminate Unnecessary Filler Words

Similarly, you want to eradicate unnecessary filler words and phrases that provide little in the way of substance. For example:

Incorrect

For all intents and purposes, it was a long day.
Needless to say, we could have performed much better.
When it really comes down to it, it's about one's own dedication.

Correct

It was a long day.
We could have performed much better.
It's about one's own dedication.

5) Be Clear and Direct

A good practice is to adopt a clearer and more direct style. Academic writing is not about creating intrigue or using technical language to try and confound your reader: it is the opposite. Do not be afraid to use short, punchy sentences. In general, it is good practice to vary your sentence lengths and certainly to avoid sentences that are too long or that run-on (see Chapter 8). If you have a sentence that looks too wordy or unwieldy, work back through it to tighten, make it more direct and use fewer words. Focus on each sentence making one main point, rather than multiple points. However, make sure that each sentence is still a complete sentence (see Chapter 8).

The same can be said for paragraph lengths. Make sure your essays have consistent paragraph lengths. Remember from Chapter 6 that each paragraph should represent another step forward in the sequence of your essay, such as discussing a specific issue or carrying out a specific component of your analysis.

By having consistent paragraph lengths, you are encouraged to ensure that each paragraph covers an appropriate level of detail in the available word space.

6) Use Effective Topic Sentences

As also discussed in Chapter 6, topic sentences are an essential aspect of good structure. They provide a valuable signal to reader about where you are taking them next in the journey. Nevertheless, you should not literally describe what is coming up next in your topic sentence and can instead convey information *as well as* signal at the same time. For example:

Incorrect

This essay will now analyze the potential problems that can occur when adopting a party-list PR system. The first of these downsides is that there is less of a direct link between MPs and their constituents.

Correct

An important downside of a party-list PR system is the loss of direct link between MPs and their constituents.

The reader will immediately know from this sentence that we are now moving on to discuss the downsides in the coming paragraph. There is no need to spell it out before you move into the substance.

7) Use an Active Voice

You might sometimes hear about the use of an active and a passive voice. Ultimately, it is about the placement of your subjects and objects in a sentence. Usually, the subject comes first and does something to an object with a verb (e.g. "The dog is black." Dog = subject, is = verb, black = object). This uses the active voice. By contrast, a passive voice will move the object to the beginning and the subject to the end, usually forcing you to add more words (e.g., "Black is the colour of the dog.").

Some further examples:
The story was written by John Smith = John Smith wrote the story.
The group had been joined by her = She joined the group.
Shock is what the audience experienced = The audience was shocked.
The experiment had been carried out by us = We carried out the experiment.

The point is that sometimes a change in the tense and layout of the sentence can make the point more direct and save words. Similarly, changing a sentence to be affirmatively worded rather than negatively worded can save words. For example:

Wordy

Unless they score more than 30, they will not be permitted to proceed to the next stage.

Concise

They must score more than 30 to proceed to the next stage.

Similarly, using noun phrases at the start of sentences can make the sentences clearer and more direct. Compare:

Wordy

If a company, through its behaviours and actions in the market, demonstrates a potential concern about risks, it could benefit from having a dedicated risk management department. Sometimes, within a risk department, the head of the department is called the Risk Director and it is this Risk Director who is responsible for monitoring and measuring risk, as well as inputting controls against risk across the organization.

Concise
Risk-averse companies should introduce a dedicated risk management department. The Risk Officer, at the head of the department, can then monitor, measure and input controls against risks across the organization.

In all cases, and as with many of these things, it is important to be clear that adopting a wordier sentence is not necessarily wrong. Depending on the flow and tone of the piece, a wordier sentence might be more appropriate or effective. However, it is worth trying to achieve conciseness wherever possible and only adding a wordier prose where it is genuinely necessary. This will make your work far more engaging, direct and easier to understand.

8) Possibly Reduce Adverbs

Adverbs often end in 'ly' and are usually adjectives (descriptive words) that are converted into a verb (doing words). For example: kindly, commonly, gracefully, desirously, actually, really, amazingly, firmly, strongly, feebly, dramatically, and so on (see Chapter 8). Many commentators suggest that these words have less of a place in academic writing and there is certainly some truth in that. In casual writing, such as this guidebook, it is *perfectly* acceptable to use adverbs *widely*. However, you may want to limit their use in academic writing. Not only do they add extra words, but they also make your work more clunky, less direct and more qualified in tone.

Incorrect
Haaman's theory is certainly and perfectly logical and is actually only really limited by the reasonably conflicting data from an earlier, timely and suitably designed study.

Correct

Haaman's theory is logical and limited only by conflicting data from one earlier study.

This is not to say that all adverbs are bad or do not have their place. Just monitor them to see if they *really* add anything to your arguments, other than clunkiness.

9) Omit Any Pointless Transitions

The powerful role of *transitional* phrases within essay structuring was discussed in Chapter 6. These phrases—like *However, That said, Despite this, Nevertheless, By contrast*, and so on—provide vital signalling to the reader and help maintain the flow and direction of the narrative. It helps the reader understand where the argument thread is going and any change of direction between steppingstones. However, when reading your work back you can often spot superfluous transitional phrases whose deletion will cause little loss to the essay's flow.

Incorrect

It is also important to note that, despite this, without certain transitional phrases the work might be just as readable. In fact, it could even be suggested that their deletion might make the work more, not less, powerful.

Correct

Without certain transitional phrases, the work might be just as readable. Their deletion could make the work more, not less, powerful.

As long as you are holding the reader's hand just enough and keeping that general direction and flow of travel going, you may not need to add transitional phrases to everything. Indeed, the substance in the sentences might steer the direction themselves.

10) Some Warnings on Technical Language and Contracted Words

There is certainly something to be said for using technical or "clever" terms that convey a lot of meaning. For example, instead of saying "This approach could offer a way to cure all issues and problems", you could say, "This approach could offer a panacea." However, there can be issues when students try to force in technical language at the expense of being clear and precise. While it is good to use a thesaurus to locate concise words that convey a lot of meaning, try to avoid selecting overly extravagant or showy words just to sound clever. The best academic writers are exceptionally clear and comprehensible. Too often we see students trying to sound clever with flashy words, but actually achieving the opposite by writing things that are muddled or unclear. As such, if you need two simpler words, as opposed to one obscure word that might cause the reader to stumble, then use the two word option!

As discussed in Chapter 8, another **very** common mistake in students' academic writing is the use of contractions, such as *can't, won't, isn't, hasn't, wouldn't, there's, they're, we're,* and so on. While these contractions are fine for casual or informal writing, they are poor practice in formal and academic settings. **Do not** use them in your essays as a word-saving technique!

11) Use Fewer and Shorter Direct Quotes

A big cause of students' over-reliance on direct quotes is a lack of confidence in their own writing or academic voice. For sure, short direct quotes can be useful, especially if they are highly illustrative or expressive. However, please do not overuse them. Where you do, you can use ellipses and square brackets to cut them down and fit them tightly within *your* narrative. Ellipses are the three dots you see (…) that represent words being omitted, whereas square brackets [ ] disclose words that convey better meaning, which are not contained in the original text.

9. Writing Approaches

For example:

Too wordy
As Smith puts it, "There is certainly much to admire about the agreement between New Labour government and the devolved nations that was negotiated in 1998. It helped define the role and responsibilities of the different parties, as well as provide an objective template against which good performance could be measured. The particular focus on the definitions provided in the opening discussions and first few segments of the agreement was a triumph" (2020, 81).

Better
According to Smith, there is "much to admire about the agreement ... negotiated in 1998." It defined everyone's roles and provided "an objective template" for measuring performance. In particular, the "focus on the definitions in the [introduction] was a triumph" (2020, 81).

It is important to reduce direct quotes and instead paraphrase the ideas and views of others. It saves a lot of words, but it also allows you to retain control of the narrative and argument. Too many direct quotes will severely impact the structure and flow of the discussion, causing it to jump around or conflict too much. Paraphrasing allows you to subtly control the discussion, as well as create certain meanings or inferences. Over-reliance on direct quotes can also imply poor understanding and knowledge on your part. A student who is well versed, well read and confident in their subject will have no problem putting things into their own words.

As an example, look at the following passages. In the first one, the narrative, structure and academic voice is completely lost. The present piece is being steered down a particular path by the narrative of *another* analysis, which is not suitable. It's also wasting a huge number of words. The second example demonstrates that removing the direct quotes controls the narrative and utilizes the material far more effectively.

Incorrect

This approach does not work because "there are things that can go wrong. Not least the reports of loneliness and a general sense of unfulfillment across the wider workforce. However, the upsides outweigh the downs. It is a highly successful approach that will uplift operators in the app coding industry. With careful monitoring and a central role of powerful and directive leadership from the top, as well as a long history of first-rate investment in technology and technological systems and tools, the approach will undoubtedly succeed. It drives up efficiency and profitability in digital-focused companies, such as design, coding, media and computer engineering, where the existing reliance on computers perfectly complements its integration" (Pullman 2023, p. 5). This approach is unlikely to be suitable for Halligan's Widgets Ltd, however, as they do not have the sufficient technological infrastructure to implement it.

Correct

This approach carries potential risks to employee well-being and motivation (Pullman 2023). More critically, it is better suited to companies that rely on extensive technological infrastructure (Smith 2023), making it likely unsuitable for Halligan's Widgets.

Students can also commonly use a direct quote incorrectly in specific areas. For example, do not directly quote information:

- ✗ That should be common knowledge. For example, "As Yamoto says, 'Barack Obama became President of the United States in 2009' (2018, 2)."

- ✗ That is not a particularly special idea. For example, "Scully informs us that, 'Obama's reign occurred between 2009-2017 and he served his two full terms as President of the United States. In that time, he governed on a wide range of issues, including Federal and overseas, with a particular focus on addressing health and wealth inequalities in the United States. He was the 44th President and had previously been a Senator for Illinois' (2019, 4)."

- ✗ That contradicts the surrounding statement in relation to it. For example, "Barack Obama was a deeply unpopular president. As Rodriguez puts it, 'He was widely praised for his approach to foreign policy, as well as his calm management of many domestic challenges' (2020, 5)."

- ✗ That does not relate to the surrounding statement. For example, "Barack Obama was a widely revered and admired president. As Hussain summarizes it, 'The Republicans dominated Congress during much of Obama's premiership' (2022, 7)."

Taking all of the above together, you can see that direct quotes should not be used freely or liberally within your work. In fact, keeping them short, direct, punchy and succinct will make your essay more effective, powerful and persuasive. It also makes it easier to read and will save you lots of wasted words in the process. Just reserve them for very short and particularly poignant phrases or words that perfectly illustrate or encapsulate a concept.

12) Focus on the Argument

The need to be hypercritical on what to include and what to exclude from your essay was discussed in detail in Chapter 3 in the context of description versus analysis. You must always be asking what detail is necessary, if any, to advance your argument. If going into lots of interesting background information is not providing *necessary* meaning for the reader, then it can probably be omitted. This is a major word-saver when it comes to being concise, as well as ensuring your essay is rich with analytical discussions and ideas. Quite often we write things and then, on review, realize that we have perhaps added more detail than is necessary. Work back through and cut down the "background information" that does little to advance the main propositions of the thesis.

One also needs to be careful not to go too far the other way. You still need to demonstrate understanding and knowledge of complex ideas, as well as explain complex or less common ideas and concepts to the reader that are pertinent to the discussion. It is a tricky balance to get right, I know! As an example from the discipline of law:

Unnecessary Words

The freedom to exercise prerogative powers in a manner contravening constitutional policy was a key factor in Miller (No 2).[13] In this case, the Prime Minister, Boris Johnson, attempted to prorogue parliament for 6 weeks during a period of constitutional crisis, while the UK was hurtling towards a 'No Deal' exit from the European Union: a so-called 'Hard Brexit'. Gina Miller, and her renowned counsel, Lord Pannick, who both had already successfully fought and won a case against Theresa May's government on executive powers in 2017, brought a case against Boris Johnson in 2019. Their primary argument was that prorogation of parliament, using royal prerogative powers now retained by the executive, contravened the core constitutional concept of parliamentary sovereignty. A key issue in the case was whether the prorogation of parliament was a legal (justiciable) matter, and within the realm of judicial intervention, or fell within the realm of political discretion (non-justiciable). The Supreme Court ruled that, given that Boris Johnson had effectively misled the Queen in his advice to prorogue parliament and clearly had an unlawful motive for doing so, the matter was thus a legal—not political—one. As such, Miller was successful in the case. The result is that, while political in essence, prerogative powers may not be exercised in a manner that contravenes essential constitutional principles, such as restricting parliamentary sovereignty or democratic accountability.

Better
Miller (No 2) affirms that the exercise of prerogative powers can be subject to judicial scrutiny when they conceivably conflict with essential constitutional principles, such as restricting parliamentary sovereignty.[17]

13) Edit and Proofread Thoroughly

I know I say this for almost everything, but that is because its importance can never be overstated. Nobody writes everything right the first time. In fact, most people do not write things correctly even when editing for the second or third time. Good work and powerful writing demand constant proofreading, checking and editing. Many of us write by pouring out all our thoughts and ideas on to the page. We get it all down and invariably use too many words. We say things in a clunky, imprecise, waffly or repetitive way, just to get it down. That is normal. You then must go back through several times to "tighten" your writing. You will need to rephrase sentences and reword your points and ideas, ensuring clarity, precision and concision.

It is often said that it is easier and takes less time to write something longer, than it does something shorter. It is easy to bash out 5,000 words in a stream of consciousness. It is not so easy to then cut those 5,000 words down to a powerful, clean and concise expression of the same ideas in 2,500 words. It is therefore often the process of refinement and polishing during several edits that converts a rough and waffly essay into a pristine and concise document. What you will often find when working through your earlier "rough" draft is that there is also a lot of unintentional repetition, which can easily be remedied. For example:

Incorrect
There are a great many advantages to using this functionality when addressing oversaturation of images. The technique provides a number of added benefits, such as sharper contrast and blur reduction.

Correct
There are many advantages to using this technique when addressing image oversaturation, including sharper contrast and blur reduction.

3. Reflective Writing

Reflective writing is a different practice to traditional essay writing. For sure, most elements of the common marking criteria in Chapter 2 are likely to remain applicable, such as hitting the brief, communication, structure, critical analysis, knowledge, use of materials and referencing. Nevertheless, the entire focus is now shifted from the development of a robust, objective and persuasive academic position, built by critiquing, assimilating and manipulating the evidence, towards the inner reflection and critique of your *own personal development*. Reflective writing is often used by academics to build in assessment for practical components on your course. Reflective assessments also teach students important skills of self-reflection and continuing professional development, which are essential tools for long-term advancement.

The most important thing to remember is that reflective writing still must be *critical*. Building on the discussions regarding analysis in Chapter 3, this means avoiding just describing events (what happened), but instead critically questioning *why* they happened and evaluating the different steps on *how* to improve in the future.

Here is a list of extremely handy tips on reflective writing. Observing these will make a huge difference to the quality of your reflective essays:

✓ **Focus on the *why, how* or *what it means*, not the *what*.**
Reflective writing should never be about just describing what has happened or explaining your experiences. It needs to go deeper than this and comprehend

what those experiences mean to *you*, what *you* have taken away from them, and what *you* will do in the future in response. Take an extreme example:

Wrong
"I walked to the shop. I found it hard to find the right kind of cake for the party because they were all so expensive. When I chose the right cake, I went to the counter. The sales assistant was so rude because he basically just ignored me. This made me angry."

Here you have only explained what happened (the "what"). This is a very poor reflection. Instead, we need to understand the why, what it all means to *you*, and the different ways that you could interpret or respond to the situation.

Correct
"I walked to the shop. Given that I am an experienced marathon runner, I found the walk particularly easy. Nevertheless, I did find boredom a particular challenge because it took so long. In future I might listen to podcasts or peaceful music while I walk. Choosing the right cake was also difficult because they were all so expensive. I found it very tricky to make all the calculations between the size of cake, its cost and the different characteristics, such as decorations, filling, nutritional information and freshness. In future I will make sure to have a clearer idea on the required specifications of the cake, including available budget and required characteristics, before setting off. When purchasing the cake, the sales assistant seemingly ignored me. This made me angry. However, on reflection, I perhaps over-reacted. While I think of myself as an extrovert and chatty person, I need to remember that not everyone is like that. In future I am going to be more patient with staff at the store."

This is quite an unusual example as it is reflecting on an everyday experience, instead of a practical academic activity or skill. However, it illustrates the point well. You can see that the first reflection just says what happened. The second reflection contains a lot more information and specifics about what it *means*, particularly to you now and in the future. You will also notice that the second example is very wordy. This is a real challenge for effective reflective writing: you should be struggling to fit all the examples, ideas and specifics in. To achieve reflective writing excellence, you therefore also need to consider all the skills of concise writing, discussed above.

✓ **Focus on the past, present and future**
The other fundamental thing you will notice from the example above is a real sense of *past, present* and *future*. Weak reflections tend to overly focus on the past, by just describing what happened. Good reflections have a strong focus on each the past, present and future. They therefore comprehend what the past events mean to you, as you stand today, as well as discuss what future actions or steps you might take to improve or build on this in the future.

✓ **Utilize the Kolb or Gibbs reflective cycles**
Structure is something that is a little bit different for reflective writing, compared to traditional essays. You probably do not even need an introduction and conclusion. What is more, instead of being centred around the development of an overarching argument running through the spine (see Chapter 6), a reflective essay tends to be chronological or sequential around the relevant *experiences*. In other words, it deals with each experience—such as an event, lesson or activity—in turn. Within each, it runs through a cycle considering what happened, what this means in the present, and what it means in the future. Two commonly used structures or reflective "cycles" that can be used to build this up are the Kolb or Gibbs reflective cycles (see further resources in Chapter 12). Unless instructed otherwise, use these for inspiration and to help you structure and enrich your reflective analyses.

9. Writing Approaches

✓ **Focus on specifics, not generalisations**

One of the most common issues I see in students' reflective essays is the use of highly generalized or non-descript language, instead of more colourful, illustrative or specific thoughts, ideas and examples. In other words, do not just say things are "good" or "bad", but explain *specifically* what makes them good or bad. Instead of, "The lesson was fun", say something like, "The lesson was fun because the tutor was very entertaining and he made us role play different characters, which was hilarious." For example:

Wrong

"I found the economics exercise challenging. Despite this, I think I performed brilliantly. I learned a lot from it and hope to be able to use this in the future."

One should be asking: Why was it challenging? Why did *you* specifically find this challenging? What would you do differently next time? Why do you think you performed brilliantly? What specifically did you do well / not so well? How have you measured success? What did you learn from it? How will you use it in the future? What applications will it have and in what parts of life? How might you act differently in the future?

Better

"I found the economics exercise challenging because it required some level of maths ability and numeracy has never been my strength. I was also unaware of an important element in the instructions because I missed a class. Nevertheless, through being tenacious and making sure that I worked earlier in the morning, when my mind was most clear, I am pleased with my focus and overall performance on the day. Moving forward, I will make sure to leave plenty of time free in the mornings leading up to an assessment, so that I have this valuable clear head space. I will also develop a better symbiotic relationship with peers, where we can keep each other informed of important things missed from class. I can

take the class learning forward too, as the microeconomic principles will help me design more effective teams in my working life."

We have now moved from just saying that things were good or simple that we "will learn from them", to explaining *why* they were good, and what *specifically* we have learned from them.

✓ **Tell, then show**

This is an adaptation of the practice of "show, don't tell". This principle is used by fiction writers to encourage them to illustrate a scene by actions and descriptive writing, rather than just bluntly stating a character's thoughts or feelings. A reverse principle can be applied to reflective writing in many ways, but where you *first identify the feeling* and *then use descriptive language* to provide deeper meaning, examples or context. For example, do not just say, "I have learned that I should actively listen." What do you mean by actively listen? Instead, say things like, "I have learned that I should actively listen, such as using engaged body language, non-verbal cues and frequent confirmatory questions."

✓ **Be selfish**

By this I mean you should try to relate everything else back to *you*. Do not just say what the tutor did, or what was in the library, or what your colleagues did. Explain what those things mean to you. It's about *your* reflection on your *own* learning.

✓ **Be critical, even if you are happy**

I have read far too many reflections that do not have a lot to say because the student has been reasonably happy and satisfied with their performance. Even if you have done amazingly well, you can *always* find things to improve on. Always. If you cannot, then you are not very good at reflection! Think about how you can do things even better, or quicker, or more efficiently, or with less mental strain, or in a way that supports others, and so on. Finding things to improve upon makes for a richer and more effective reflection, even if you are shoehorning it in.

✓ **Use wider reading**

Excellent reflections will make use of wider resources and materials. Just because it is a reflective account does not mean that your skills of sourcing useful theories or evaluating different solutions should be repressed. In fact, the richer and denser you can make your reflective account with references to wider materials, the better. For example, if you say you are going to improve on time management in the future, then pull some specific steps from a guide on time management and refer to this. For example, "To do this I will follow steps set out by McKeanney, which include more effective use of my calendar and building in more breaks and rewards." This shows you have not just reflected on what has not worked but have got on with trying to fix it by reading lots of guidance.

It is important when referring to wider literature and materials to still be specific. Do not just say, "I will refer to Martin's excellent comprehensive guide on academic essays." Say which specific steps or components you are taking away from this book to address an identified weakness. For example, "I will adopt Martin's fish skeleton structure, to help me strengthen the central thread running through my essays." This shows not only that you have a clear plan to fix it but, as importantly, you have also read the source!

10. Referencing

1. The Importance of Referencing

All high-quality research publications—be it government reports, peer-reviewed articles or published monographs—will reference the sources used to conduct their analyses and reach their conclusions. The reasons for this are manifold. It provides a useful reference for readers of your work, who can conduct further research through the links provided. It makes the work more persuasive and robust, by allowing readers to locate the source material and verify the accuracy of its incorporation. It signifies to the reader that the researcher has done their homework and covered key sources in producing their work. Most importantly, it provides the necessary attribution to other authors and researchers to ensure that their work, data or ideas are not passed off as your own. This is why referencing is such an important aspect of academic writing and why we impose the requirement upon you. Ultimately, it is to ensure that your academic work is persuasive, objective, reliable, trustworthy and not the result of plagiarism.

Many students become panicked about referencing at some stage in their studies. I think a large part of this is how it is explained—or not explained—at most institutions. Sometimes students seem to develop the view that, unless they reference properly, they will lose a lot of grades or could even face significant sanctions. This creates anxiety in many students and a fear that slightly putting their foot wrong will cause them to be penalized or their work to be downgraded. I have got two pieces of good news for you.

First, weak referencing should not normally lead to a significant reduction in your grade. While it can still have an impact, unless it raises critical questions of academic honesty, it is likely to have less impact than other assessment criteria (see Chapter 2). The second piece of good news is that referencing is incredibly easy! Most students new to academic study will be panicked at first, but before long will relax into it, finding it all reasonably natural and untaxing. This handy chapter gives you all the things you need to know, and you will hopefully see that referencing—although incredibly important to get right—is quite straightforward.

2. Footnotes and In-Text Citations

It is important to first establish two distinctive styles of citing materials within an essay: footnotes and in-text. Footnote citations are more commonly used in disciplines such as humanities, law and languages. They involve the insertion of a numerical sequence of footnote numbers into the main text in superscript, like this,[1] which are then linked at the foot (bottom) of the page with the reference. For many, it is a neat and attractive method of referencing materials, as it prevents the main body from becoming too clunky. Instead of having lots of author names, brackets, years, page numbers, and extra words, you just have occasional numbers in small superscript. Better yet, the references inside each citation are available at the bottom of the page, instead of in a separate reference list at the back of the essay.

Nevertheless, in-text citations are the most common method of referring to materials. It is found in most other disciplines and particularly across the sciences. This is where the authors of the source are entered immediately after the relevant point inside brackets, along with the year, e.g., (Smith 2023). If the source is a direct quote, the reference should include a page range, e.g., (Smith 2023, pp. 3-5). The citations must be backed up by a bibliography or reference list at the end of the essay which lists full references for all the sources organized in alphabetical order by author.

How to Cite Sources

This subsection will give some important practice points and tips on how to cite sources between footnote and in-text referencing. The specific rules of different referencing styles (e.g., APA, Harvard, Chicago, MLA, OSCOLA) are discussed in the last section.

Footnotes

✓ **Use Ctrl + Alt + F in Word or Command + Option + F in Pages**

Many students coming to footnote citations for the first time understandably do not know the useful functionality that is already built into their word processor. Your word processor will automatically compile your footnote list for you if you use the above key shortcuts to insert a footnote.

✓ **Insert footnotes after punctuation**

This one is important! Not all tutors are strict about it, but others can feel their blood pressure growing if they see repeated requests to remedy this not addressed. I am one of those tutors. If using standard superscript numbers, as opposed to the less common numbers in square brackets, you **must** insert the footnote number *after* all punctuation. Yes, that means *after* full stops and *after* commas and *after* speech marks. The *only* punctuation exception is when citing inside parentheses (like this[55]). Please note:

Wrong!
- As explained by Smith and Pullman, "this is bad practice[32]."
- Please **do not** do this when inserting footnotes[156], as some tutors will find it infuriating[157].

Correct
- As explained by Smith and Pullman, "this is good practice."[32]

- Please do this when inserting footnotes,[156] otherwise your tutors will get very frustrated.[157]

✓ **Use consistent formatting in reference fields**

One of the most common problems I see with footnote-based citations is inconsistent formatting in the footnotes. Your entire footer throughout the document needs to be in consistent font, text size and line spacing throughout. The only formatting distinction should be italicized and non-italicized text or, possibly, a hyperlink for URLs. Everything else must be identical. Frequently enter Ctrl + A in the footer (to select *all* text across the footer) and then select the correct font, size and line spacing. The line spacing is normally 1.0, the text is usually the same font as the main body and the text size is usually one or two steps smaller than the main body.

✓ **Use numbers, not letters or Roman numerals**

Unless specifically instructed otherwise, use number sequencing for your footnotes (1, 2, 3, etc). Please do not use letters (a, b, c) or Roman numerals (i, ii, iii). It's not cool or stylish. It is just clunky, erratic and harder to decipher.

✓ **Do not insert multiple footnotes at the same point**

Very often I have seen students insert multiple footnotes at the same point in the essay, to add multiple sources. (For example, like this.[16][17][18]) You should just insert *one* footnote at any particular point and instead put all the applicable sources under the same footnote field, usually separated by a semicolon (;). (The citation being like this.[16])

✓ **Put a period at the end of each reference field**

The reference field is the space in your footer that comes after each number in the list. It is where you add your references: usually one per footnote number, although it can be more than one source separated by semicolons. Once each reference field is finished, you must add a period.

✓ Use Ibid and Supra

To avoid having identical references repeated over and over in the footnotes, academics insert the word 'Ibid' or 'Id' to repeat the same source in the footnote immediately above, or 'Supra or 'Op Cit' plus the relevant footnote number to identify an already referenced source located earlier in the document. For example:

> 11. John Smith (2023) *Referencing Correctly*. 2nd Edn. Oxford: Oxford University Press.
> 12. Belinda Pullman (2022), 'How to Cite Materials: A Bibliographic Perspective', *Journal of Academic Practices*, 13(4), pp. 34-48.
> 13. Ibid, p. 37. [This refers to Pullman article, at page 37.]
> 14. Supra, Smith, Note 11. [This refers to Smith book found at Footnote 11.]

✓ Practice using cross-referencing functionality in your word processor

This was a miracle discovery for me and is something that no one else I have met seems to know about! Why it's not wider knowledge, I am not sure. When using Ibid or Supra to cross-reference a previous source, use the 'Cross-Referencing' functionality in your word processor. Numbers and the location of sources inevitably change as your essay takes shape. In our example, while the Pullman article might be immediately above footnote 13 at the moment, or the Smith article located at footnote 11, this could very easily change later if text is moved, deleted or edited, or if new footnotes are inserted that put all the other numbers out.

Keeping an eye on these changing numbers manually is a nightmare and prone to making constant errors. Therefore, whenever you are inserting an Ibid or Supra reference, go to the 'References' tab in Word, then select 'Cross-Reference', then select 'Footnote' from the dropdown menu. From here, insert the specific footnote number you are cross-referring back to. Then Word will automatically change the number for you if anything moves around.

In-text

✓ **If the author is mentioned in the text, just put the year in brackets**

If you are citing an author whose name is already part of the passage of text, then you only need to add the year. For example, "According to Smith (2023), this is the correct way to do things." Similarly, if inserting a direct quote with the name and year already in the passage, you only need the page range in brackets. For example, "As Smith and Pullman said in 2023, 'this is correct' (p. 2)."

✓ **Make note of comma placement and page range requirements**

Just a minor point, but different institutions and publishers have different expectations regarding the use of a comma in the brackets, as well as the presentation of the page range. Examples of different combinations include: (Smith 2023, pp. 5-6) / (Smith 2023, 5-6) / (Smith, 2023, pp. 5-6) / (Smith, 2023, 5-6) / (Smith 5-6). Take note of whether there is a comma between the author and year, or a "p." before the page numbers. The last example, without a year or any commas, is only seen in MLA-style citations.

✓ **Insert parentheses before punctuation, except within quotations**

By contrast with footnotes, in-text citation parentheses are entered before punctuation (i.e., *before* full stops, commas and close brackets). The only exception is when the reference is being inserted for a quote, in which case the brackets will appear after the quotation. This is because everything inserted *inside* a quotation which is not in square brackets, like [this], is an exact copy of the quote.

Wrong!
This is *not* where we insert citation brackets. (Smith 2023) As Pullman reminds us, 'the reference needs to be connected to the sentence' in which it appears, so this is wrong. (Pullman 2022, p. 5).

Correct
This is where we really should insert citation brackets (Smith 2023). As Pullman reminds us, 'the reference needs to be connected to the sentence' in which it appears (Pullman 2022, p. 5).

✓ **Use 'et al' if more than 3 authors**

If the source has up to three authors, then name them within the parentheses. For example, (Smith, Pullman and Bates, 2023). Also make sure to use the full word "and" between authors, instead of an ampersand (&). If there are four or more (e.g., Smith, Pullman, Bates *and* Higgins, 2023), then just put the first author followed by 'et al'. In this example, (Smith et al, 2023).

✓ **Add a, b, c to the year if there is more than one source with the same name and year**

For example, if you have two articles by Smith in the year 2023, then it is not going to be clear which source is being referenced if the citation says (Smith 2023). To resolve this, we create multiples of Smith in 2023 by adding letters. For example, (Smith 2023a) and (Smith 2023b) and so on.

✓ **If author is unclear, put the publisher**

References are organized and alphabetized by author name. However, sometimes a source may not have a clear natural person as an author. In such cases, use the publishing organization or name of the publication. A common one is newspaper articles, where the journalist's name might not be shown. In such cases, use the name of the newspaper (i.e., the publication). Another one is reports or publications by organizations which are not attributed to the author. In such cases, put the name of the organization.

Both footnotes and in-text
✓ **Do not bother getting the specific referencing correct until the end**
When busy putting your essay together, the last thing you want to be doing is worrying about the fiddly process of referencing according to a specific style. When working in draft form, keep your references in draft form also, helping you to keep your writing pace going. You still need to insert a citation with the author's name and page range (if needed). Otherwise, you won't remember where you got the source from. However, do not worry about getting the reference itself into the correct layout and format, with all the necessary components, until the end. At the end you can swiftly work through, just entering the source into Google Scholar (scholar.google.com), clicking 'Cite', and then copying all the details (like year, volume and issue number, publisher, page location, etc) across. Then you can edit these into the correct format all together.

✓ **Practice using referencing software, if you can**
Many people swear by referencing software like **EndNote** (endnote.com) or **Mendeley** (mendeley.com). These super handy programs automatically synchronize all your documents and materials with your chosen word processor, as well as automatically generate and store your citations for you. I know so many people who are delighted that they made the switch and began using a program like this. If you are in academic studies for a few more years or you are a practising academic yourself, then the benefits of learning to use such a program will probably far outweigh the time spent getting used to it. In such cases, I would probably recommend **EndNote** for its ease of use.

10. Referencing

✓ **Do not add materials to your reference list or bibliography that are not referenced in the essay**

Do not add references to your reference list or bibliography unless they are specifically referenced or cited in the essay. It should not serve as a list of materials generally used in your research; instead, it should be a list of materials you have specifically *incorporated* into your essay.

✓ **Remove quoted direct page ranges in bibliography**

All the materials and sources in your final bibliography or reference list should be listed as the *whole* sources. Make sure to delete any specific page ranges you might have used within the source. For example, if in your essay you use a direct quote from a textbook and then identify that you copied it from pages 456-457, do not include (pp. 456-457) in your bibliography. This would only go in the parentheses (for in-text citations) or in the footnote (for footnotes), but not in the bibliography.

✓ **Use 'Sort Ascending' to organize bibliography**

For ease of reference, it is crucial that your reference list or bibliography is organized by author name alphabetically. Once again, your word processor has the tools to do this automatically, saving you a huge amount of time and removing the possibilities for error. Just highlight all the sources and then select 'Sort Ascending', which will organize them from A → Z.

✓ **Refer to sources inside sources**

If you find you are repeating the same source a lot, you might want to look for sources within that source, to make the same point but with a different reference. This makes you look more well-read than you might in fact be! Relatedly, if the source is a low-quality source (see Chapter 4) or something like Wikipedia, you want to try and find high-quality sources within that source, that show greater reliability and quality. Never cite Wikipedia or super low-quality sources, such as a site called something like QuickEssayAnswers.net!

When to Cite Sources

The next question is *when* to provide evidence that is backed up with a citation. In other words, if we make a statement in our essay, when do we know that it needs a reference to wider material? The short answer is whenever you have used a source as evidence or in the development of ideas. This includes when you draw on the views, analyses or arguments of others. Of course, it can be a little more complex than this. Here are some handy tips to help you decide when you need a reference:

- ✓ **If using a direct quote or copying anything from anywhere, you must reference**

An obvious time that you must add a reference is whenever you use a direct quote of someone else. Any content that is coped-and-pasted from elsewhere **must** be placed within quotation marks and have a reference including the specific page from where it was taken.

- ✓ **You should reference any data or statistics**

If making a statement that includes data or statistics, you need to identify the source of those statistics. For example, if you said, "88% of people are left-handed" or "There are an estimated 100 million sharks killed by human activities every year", these would need a source.

- ✓ **If mentioning someone else's ideas by name, then they need to be referenced**

For example, if you said, "According to Whelan, gender-based roles are indoctrinated early in childhood." Then of course you need to add a reference to the source where Whelan discussed this.

10. Referencing

✓ **If making a factual assertion that is not common knowledge, it might need to be referenced**

For example, if you said, "Gender-based roles are indoctrinated early in childhood", like the Whelan statement in the previous example, then you should probably still cite Whelan. This is because it is making a factual assertion and one that likely needs verification. This is a tricky area as it can be hard to determine what is a factual assertion and what is a more general statement or widely accepted idea. In some ways, it is also a matter of choice whether to reference these or not. For example, our example above may not *need* referencing, but would probably benefit from it if we are looking to be *persuasive and reliable*. Through lots of practice and conscious reading, you will begin getting a sense of the kinds of statements that are factual assertions that would benefit from being backed up by a reference.

✓ **If unsure, add a reference**

The first thing to say, as was noted in Chapter 2, is that you are likely to be better served adding more sources, rather than less. It makes your work look well researched and thorough, while giving you an air of authority. So, if weighing up whether to add a reference or not, err on the side of adding it, rather than not.

3. Referencing Styles

It is beyond the focus of this book to write a detailed explanation of all the different referencing styles and their precise differences in terms of layout. You can use a reference generator, such as CiteThisForMe, BibGuru or Scribbr, to get examples of the distinct yet small variations between all these different styles. To help understand the huge range of styles, this table shows some examples around the world, as well as some of the disciplines they are commonly adopted in.

Referencing Style	Commonly found in...
APA (American Psychological Association)	Psychology, Social Sciences, Education, Nursing, Economics, Business, Physics
MLA (Modern Language Association)	Language, Linguistics, Humanities, Philosophy
Harvard	Biology, Chemistry, Sciences, Archaeology, Social Sciences, Business
Vancouver	Medicine, Biology, Chemistry, Health Sciences
Chicago	Literature, History, Arts
Bluebook	Law (United States)
OSCOLA	Law (United Kingdom)
AMS (American Mathematical Society)	Mathematics

10. Referencing

MHRA (Modern Humanities Research Association)	Humanities, Media
IEEE (Institute of Electrical and Electronics Engineers)	Electronics, Engineering, Computer Science

Many students might rightly ask, "Why does it really matter? As long as I am putting in enough information to locate the sources, surely that is enough?" Sorry to say, but it matters to academics because it just matters to us! The way I often see it is that we are testing a student's ability to decipher instructions. All the guidance and information you could need is available on each referencing style. If you cannot follow those instructions, such as understanding where to put commas or use italics in a reference, then it speaks volumes about your ability to read, interpret and apply simple instructions, as well as your attention to detail. Indeed, academics have the same responsibility to match the house style of any publisher when we submit books or journals for publication. It also matters because it is about disciplinary practice, familiarity, consistency and neatness. If all scholars in a discipline are using familiar styles, it makes it easier and quicker for academics in that world to understand, digest and assimilate materials. So, simply, it just matters.

That said, as mentioned in the outset, we are unlikely to *significantly* downgrade a paper because it failed to follow minute technical requirements of the required referencing style. At least not earlier in your studies when you are familiarizing yourself with referencing. However, as your academic work progresses, we expect to see greater conformity, accuracy and consistency in the quality of your referencing. Worry not, as I have some super useful tips for you:

✓ **Be careful with reference generators**

Across the web now you can often find reference generators where you fill in the requisite information and it generates a formatted reference for you. Similarly, you might select "Cite" on something like Google Scholar or the online journal to get a generated reference. These systems can generate useful references for you to *adapt*, but in my experience, they are frequently wrong in their layout or get muddled between different data fields. If you find one that works well and you have double-checked it across multiple sources and it still hits it spot on every time, then great! More likely, you can use reference generators to play around with formatting changes or to speed up the process by converting data into a closer format more quickly. In all cases, references will still need a visual check for accuracy after they have been generated.

✓ **Focus on the tiny details likes italics, commas, brackets, spaces and periods**

It may seem pedantic but, as mentioned, it is also a test of your attention to detail. It shows poor attention to detail if you should use period in your reference but use commas instead. Or, if you should italicize the publication, but italicize the article name instead. It's pedantic, but you still have to get it right. Pay very close attention to the specific punctuation and formatting used and when. And, by close attention, I mean *close*. Not *close enough*!

✓ **It is mostly about the common source types**

It is easy to get panicked about all the different referencing layouts for different source types, from eBooks, to web sources, to official reports, to television programmes. Each of these might have their own way of being referenced that needs to be done right. However, in reality, there is probably only a handful of source types that you will use 95% of the time. These are likely to include books, journal articles, reports, web sources and chapters in edited volumes. If you really master these, then that is most of the work done. Referencing these main source types will soon become quick and easy. You may rarely use an unfamiliar source type, like an online lecture or a radio broadcast, but you can deal with these individually as they arise. Most of your referencing will be from the standard academic sources above.

✓ **Make frequent reference to the referencing style guide**

Do not assume that after reading the style guide that you know it. I have used some referencing styles for years and still, to this day, keep the style guide open in a browser tab when I am doing my referencing.

✓ **Observe bibliography or reference list formatting styles**

Do not just assume that you can compile the bibliography or reference list how you please. In some cases, there will be widespread or expected practices around the use of bullet points or hyphens, line spacing, formatting and overall layout. In some disciplines, you may even be expected to separate out the source types into several lists under various subheadings (e.g., Web Sources, Articles, Media, etc). As with everything, make sure the bibliography is also neat and consistently formatted.

✓ **Note some common conventions**

This chapter has covered various conventions that are commonly observed, such as the inclusion of a page range when adding a direct quote. Note some other common referencing conventions:

- The reference list usually has the author's surname first and is organized alphabetically. Their other names will then follow behind a comma, either in full or abbreviated to their first letters with a period for each.

- The title of journals and books are *usually* italicized, whereas the articles or chapter titles within them are in quotation marks.

- Although not universal, the year of publication is usually placed in parentheses and often comes second after the author(s) name.

- Volume and issue numbers of journal articles are rarely displayed with words. For example, it is rarely Vol. 3 Iss. 1 and more commonly 3(1).

- You do not include a web address (URL) for every source. In many cases, sources such as journal articles, books and chapters should be referenced without any URL.

✓ **If it's a very obscure source type, then making a good guess is fine**

In 99% of cases, you will find the format of the specific source type. However, sometimes there might be an very unusual or obscure source type that is not listed under your referencing style guide. This is particularly common with primary source materials, that are not archived or documented in the same way as many research materials we might more commonly use. In such rare cases, you can just use an educated guess based on your understanding of how the style is usually set out or approached. For example, one of my law students once asked me how they should cite a case from the Bahía Court of Justice in Brazil. As an English lawyer and academic, I am not proficient in the finer intricacies of the Brazilian judicial system: I certainly would never downgrade a student on their accuracy. I told the student to just copy how the Brazilians cite the case!

✓ **Consistency is king**

While we expect you to adopt the specific requirements of your assigned referencing style, we are not likely to lose sleep if you slightly moderate it to lose a space somewhere or to use a comma instead of a period somewhere else. What would be more problematic would be if you did this *inconsistently*. Model your references on your assigned style and, more than anything, make sure all of your reference formats (as applied to each specific source type) are the same. If you have used single quotation marks around journal article titles in one reference, make sure to do that for all other journal article references.

✓ **Pay close attention to feedback**

It might seem obvious, but it never ceases to amaze me how poorly many students do at this. If your tutor has made any comments or corrections on your referencing, then do not just scan over it and forget it. Look closely at what they have told you and make sure you follow it when you are next writing an essay. I have had too many students where I will correct all of their references and associated formatting in one essay, only to get the same errors again in the next one, and then again in the third one. Each time, my frustration gets more intense, and their marks get lower. If you get feedback, use it (see Chapter 1 on this).

✓ **Practice makes perfect**

It is genuinely the case that once you get the hang of referencing, it is really quite easy. The sooner you start putting care into doing it correctly and practising the style, the sooner you will be able to do it quickly and with ease, as well as enjoy doing it too.

11. Formatting

1. The Principles of Good Formatting

Formatting refers to overall presentation issues like font types, text sizes, line spacing, paragraph spacing, margins, text colours, underlining, font effects, numbering, punctuation consistency, file management, images, tables, layout and much more. Careful formatting will make a truly momentous difference to your essay's quality. It is also incredibly simple as a step. Despite this, a properly formatted essay is a rare sight. Most students seemingly either place little value on it or they struggle with it. It is time for you to change that.

Poor formatting has all sorts of significant impacts on your work. It makes your work look amateur, unprofessional and, thus, weak. It signals that you have a lack of attention to detail, or even a lack of care or interest. It makes the work look rushed and informal, severely impacting its persuasiveness. It makes the work feel messy and unstructured, so can frustrate or disappoint the reader. It also signifies an inability to follow instructions, because there are clear rules and principles you need to be following. Therefore, read this quick and easy chapter—and refer back to it when formatting your essay—to transform your essay from a jagged lump into a pristine diamond.

Let us first consider some vitally important principles of formatting, which speak to broader formatting good practice.

- ✓ **Follow your instructions!**
It might be that your institution or department has widely expected or required formatting rules and principles. If so, stick to them. This should certainly be the case if you receive direct feedback asking you to do so. Indeed, consider whether any instructions are firm or whether they represent guidelines. For example, many

courses might encourage students to write in sans serif fonts, like Arial or Calibri, to promote readability. Nevertheless, students can in reality use any professional looking font, including serif fonts, like Times New Roman or Georgia. The main concern is usually that students use a professional looking font that is clearly legible: not something like **GOUDY STOUT**. The same goes for font size and line spacing. Sometimes instructions say 12px or 2-line spacing. However, sometimes this is a loose guideline, rather than a strict requirement. I personally opt for 12x size, 1.5-line spacing and a classic serif font like Times New Roman. It does not really matter, as long as it is professional looking and practical. Therefore, 8px fonts and 0.7-line spacing are out! Make a judgement about how firm any instructions are. The most important thing, however, is to remain professional, consistent and neat.

✓ **Aim for professionalism**
Weak formatting looks amateur, thus weakening the quality and strength of your essay. A professional looking piece gives a sense of seriousness, reliability, quality and strong provenance. When focusing on the formatting and layout of your essay, have professionalism in mind. For example, look at how formal letters, academic articles or official documents are formatted. This means choosing a professional looking font and stylings throughout. Consider also what professionalism looks like in your discipline. There might even be popular styles adopted by leading publishers and books in your discipline, or a widely adopted house style. I often feel, for example, that scientific disciplines tend to be written in sans serif fonts, whereas humanities and arts tend to be written in serif fonts. But, as always, it depends on your field!

✓ **The key is consistency**
Formatting is really all about consistency. As long as it is reasonably professional and conveys the requisite information, it does not really matter the precise formatting you choose. More important is that you stick to it rigidly throughout.

11. Formatting

Do not move from using single quotation marks to double, or from black font to charcoal font, or from numbering in Roman numerals to traditional numerals. It is therefore about weeding out formatting errors and mistakes, ensuring that they are swept up and brought into line with the rest of the document.

✓ **Always do a formatting sweep at the end**

When writing your essay, you can certainly be formatting as you go. It's good to have a formatting check occasionally, such as checking you are using consistent formatting or stylistic approaches throughout. However, it is also vital to leave a dedicated moment at the end to check everything is consistent, neat and in accordance with the intended style. At this stage, 'Select All' (Ctrl + A on Word or Cmd + A on Pages) and 'Find' (Ctrl + F on Word or Cmd + F on Pages) are your friend. As covered below.

✓ **'Select All' is especially useful for capturing the whole document**

At the very end, do a 'Select All' (Ctrl + A on Word or Cmd + A on Pages) across the whole document and choose the right font type, font size, font colour, paragraph (line spacing) and page alignment settings (see more on these below). This will automatically shift *everything* into a consistent format across these settings. Of course, some things might then need to be manually changed back. For example, the title will want to go back to being centre-aligned. However, you can at least be confident that the rest of the document is all now in the same format.

If using footnotes, you should also do the same across the entire footer field. This will ensure that all your footnotes are also consistent across these settings. This is important as footnote fields are usually littered with messy and inconsistent formats. Alternatively, you might apply 'Styles' in the main document (e.g., 'Normal', 'Title', 'Heading 1'), which would address these consistency points.

Even here, however, you must still make sure to check all the text is correctly applied to the correct style.

✓ **'Find' is very useful for fixing common errors**
If you have realized that you are frequently formatting or spelling a particular word incorrectly, you can perform a 'Find' (Ctrl + F on Word or Cmd + F on Pages) to locate all instances of the word to check or correct them. It is not just words; it could include punctuation, referencing or number errors as well. There is also the super-useful option of 'Find and Replace' (Ctrl + H on Word or Cmd + H on Pages), which can automatically change words. For example, say you have discovered that you have been referring to "periods" as "full stops" and want to switch them all over: perform a 'Find and Replace' and watch as you click through and satisfyingly change all of them in just seconds.

As another example, I am used to writing in the style of English that uses "ise", instead of "ize". For example, "realised" or "organize". With this book, however, I am aiming for a more international version of British English, so I performed a "Find" at the end of my writing for all instances of *ise, isi, isa* and *lyse*, which helped me detect words where I forgot to use the "z". For example, I spotted where I had written "analyse" and changed it to "analyze". Doing these searches, I ended up making about 50 corrections!

2. Formatting Rules to Follow

Here is a list of extremely useful tips, pointers and instructions for effective essay formatting:

✓ **Use only one font throughout**
It looks extremely messy and confusing if an essay has more than one font. Use one font and stick to it. You can enlarge the title heading and put other headings in bold, without the need to change the font. If using footnotes, you can shrink

11. Formatting

the font size by 1px or 2px. But, in all cases, you want to mostly maintain the same font. The only rare exception might be text within a table or graph, but even this should ideally be the same font too if possible.

✓ **Pay close attention to font shade**
It should go without saying that all of your text wants to be the same colour. Nevertheless, it is amazing how many students submit essays with the font subtly shifting shades. If you look at the available font colours in your word processor, you will see that there are about 30 shades of blackish-to-grey. Many of the dark charcoal type colours can be barely noticeable in difference to standard black font: but they are still noticeable! I always highlight when a student has changed shade in colours and, to me, it looks extremely messy and poor. It also suggests that a student has copied–and–pasted materials from elsewhere. As above, do 'Select All' across all of your text and make sure to choose Black (or Automatic) as the font colour.

✓ **Use *italics* to emphasize words and for foreign language**
If you really want to *emphasize* a word in a sentence, you can use italics. Like *this*. This can be particularly useful if a word essential to the sentence's meaning is getting lost in the sentence, so requires stronger contrast. For example, "Notably, this was prevalent not just among the larger species, but across *all* species under observation." Try not to over-use italics in this way. The targeted words will lose their emphasis if used too often, and it will make the work messy and hard to read. Just use it occasionally, where necessary to deliver specific meaning.

Some other common uses of italics include:
   o   When using foreign words that are not assimilated into English. For example, *déjà vu* or *Grundnorm*.

- When citing the title to works, such as books, films and articles, such as "My favourite movie is *Jaws*."

- Italics are also used for words when talking about the word specifically. For example, "The word *vax* was perhaps one of the least surprising entries into the dictionary for 2020."

- Two discipline-specific uses are when referring to genus and species names in biology (e.g., *Homo ergaster* or *Streptococcus pneumoniae*) or legal cases in law (e.g., *Donoghue v Stevenson*).

- Finally, as emphasized in Chapter 10, italics are essential in many academic referencing conventions and usually identify the title to the publication in which the source appears.

✓ Use consistent line spacing and line breaks

Line spacing is how squashed all the lines are together going vertically down the page. A good, standard line spacing is 1.5, although anything in the region of 1.0-2.0 should be okay. The main thing, again, is being consistent throughout. There may also be certain elements—such as under subheadings or in indented lists—where you have set customized spacing 'After' or 'Before' that line. This is fine, but again be consistent throughout the document. The same thing applies to line breaks (empty space) between blocks and sections. Except where using a specifically required style, in most cases you need to have an empty line break (blank space) between the end of one paragraph and the start of another. If you do not have that, you will need a clear indentation for the first line in paragraphs. Whatever you do in terms of line breaks and full line spaces between content, just be consistent from beginning to end.

11. Formatting

✓ **Do not use underline—anywhere**

I cannot think of a single part of an essay that should have underlining. Underlining is an old practice that just does not look good with modern writing technology. It is considered bad practice and unattractive to underline titles and headings. It is definitely unattractive to underline anything in the main body too. Even URLs, if included as a weblink in an essay's bibliography say, could probably have the underlining removed (just retaining the dark blue shade to emphasize the fact that it's a live link). However, your assigned referencing style for your bibliography may define how links are to be included.

✓ **Do not use bold anywhere, except in headings**

I cannot think of another area in your essay—beyond the title, headings or subheadings—where bold could belong. Of course, if you have specific instructions on where you must use bold, that is different. If not, you should limit it to your headings and subheadings. If you need to, use italics for emphasis in the main body.

✓ **Use larger font sizes for titles and headings**

There are different stylistic approaches for how you display your title and headings. I do not want to be too prescriptive. That said, slightly increasing the size of your title and your main headings allows you to emphasize them without having to add additional word effects. I recommend something like 16px for your essay title and 14px for headings, with 12px for your main text. Although you can adjust these all up and down, if preferred. I also recommend putting your section headings in bold, with the essay title not in bold; but this might be personal preference. Subheadings, if you do have any, should be the same size as the main text and might be in italics or both bold and italics.

✓ **Use consistent page alignment**

Unless told otherwise, you are free to make your essay left aligned or justified. Justified is when the words stretch across left-to-right so that the words are straight down both margins at the side; left alignment is where the text is plush to the left margin but is uneven down the right-hand margin. Left aligned has consistent spacing between words; justified expands or shrinks spaces accordingly. As always, just use one and stick to it. Although you may, of course, make your essay title centre aligned. Tables or images may be centre aligned too.

✓ **Do you use one space or two spaces after periods?**

Either is fine. Common practice these days seems to be a single space following a period, so if that is what you do, that is fine. However, if you are like me and grew up being taught to put two spaces after a full stop, stick to your guns if you want—I have! As always, the main thing is being consistent. An area that needs attention, for example, is where you have copied and pasted content from elsewhere into a direct quote. Your word processor may not flag it if suddenly a section of text has double space, but the rest does not, or vice versa.

✓ **Use a numbering system for sections and subsections, if you have them**

It might seem obvious, but if you are going to have sections and subsections, then you will want to have a consistent, neat and appropriate numbering and ordering system. Unless you are specifically instructed to follow a particular numbering system, look at examples or follow a stylistic guide for inspiration on professional styles of section numbering. Make sure this is neat and done consistently. A common numbering system is numerical digits with a period for main section headings (e.g. "1. Introduction: Decoding Solipsism") and then numerical digits with a bracket for subheadings (e.g. "1) Egocentrism and Narcissism in Clinical Studies").

11. Formatting

✓ **Do not use bullet point lists**

When it comes to *planning* your essay, as discussed in Chapter 4, then by all means use all the bullet points you need. However, in the final essay it is considered bad practice to use bullet points. Essays normally need to be written in a free-flowing narrative, where it sounds as if the writer is talking through the issues and properly explaining them. Bullet points, on the other hand, are a technique for listing bite-sized bits of information in shorthand. (As always, if instructed otherwise, follow your instructions!) It is feasible to use numbered ordering (e.g., (1), (2) and (3)) in your work, although these are better reserved for the numbering of your main sections and subsections.

✓ **Unless you are in the United States, do not put periods after abbreviations or inside acronyms**

In the United States, you will often end abbreviations with periods (e.g., Mrs. / Mr. / Dr. / Jr. / Capt. / Prof.), whereas in British English you omit the period (Mrs / Mr / Dr / Jr / Capt / Prof). In the US, acronyms with lower case letters will have periods between the letters (e.g., i.e., c.f., a.m., p.m., e.g.). In the UK, this is optional, although often done without the periods. Most other acronyms in US English are written without periods, although some US styles and approaches still promote periods inside acronyms (e.g., R.S.V.P., A.C.M.E., U.S., U.K., U.S.S.R., Ph.D.). In the UK, this is never the case (RSVP, ACME, US, UK, USSR, PhD).

✓ **Use consistent dialect**

I have discussed how I am changing all the *ise*'s to *ize*'s throughout this book. Each is a perfectly legitimate form of English language. Where I would fail, however, would be in not being consistent. Whichever form of language or dialect you choose, make sure to be consistent throughout. I have often seen students write sentences like, "It is important to recognize the importance of organisational culture." This is conflicting two different styles because *both* words should either use a "z" *or* an "s". Make sure that whatever form of dialect you choose, be it British English, US English or another form of English, you stick to it from beginning to end. As above, use Ctrl + F to locate all areas where you might have entered the wrong word and change it to be consistent.

✓ **Make sure to check all quotes and parentheses are fully paired**

It was mentioned in Chapter 10 that I all too frequently see quotations that do not close or it's not even clear where they in fact opened. I also constantly see parentheses (brackets) that do not successfully pair up and close. Check these when formatting or proofreading.

✓ **Use consistent quotation marks**

It is usually acceptable to use *either* single quotation marks (' ') or double quotation marks (" "). The main thing is to stick to the same format for the same context throughout. For example, you may have used double quotations for direct quotes and single quotations for quotes within quotes. In which case, stick to this format. There are less formal rules in terms of using quotation marks for emphasis within the main body, like "this". For example, quotation marks can be helpful to signify that a word is particularly unusual or specific to the context. For example, 'Without such "introverted norms", the character is unlikely to be viewed in such a positive light.' However, try not to over-use them and, where you do use them, try as much as possible to be consistent. *Italics* should be the main method of providing emphasis.

✓ **You might want to consider putting numbers as written words when stating 0-10, but as number characters when above 10**

This is a stylistic thing and it's not always strictly expected and, in many cases, different styles might be used. Nevertheless, if you are uncertain whether to write out a number (e.g., one, two, three, etc) or put the numerical character (e.g., 1, 2, 3, etc), then a good *starting point* is to write the word when it is between 0-10 and use numbers when it is over 10. For example, "There are seven authors who have published a whole book on this topic, while there are around 1,800 articles on Google Scholar with the words in the title." Nevertheless, this is purely a stylistic thing. I might personally use the number "7" here, so that it has a clearer contrast with the number of articles. But, naturally, if I was referring to the "two" authors who wrote a specific book, I would refer to them using the word "two". Of course, you must always use the number characters: when explaining a range (e.g., 2-6 or 342-343); when using them for number sequencing, such as section, chapter or footnote numbers; within formulae or equations; or when referring to currency (e.g., €4,000).

✓ **Images must include a caption that labels the image and discloses its origin**

In many disciplines, images are a rare sight in essays. They may be present in creative disciplines or practical scientific disciplines. An image should not really be included for general decoration or intrigue, but specifically to advance the argument. An example might be if analysis was being carried out on a particular painting or you were including a photograph of a landscape that is illustrative of the point you are making. When including images, provide them all with a caption that covers three things: their number (Figure 1, Figure 2, etc); their title (e.g., "*Sunflowers* (Oil on Canvas) – Van Gogh 1888" or "Excavation Floor Grid at Site 3 (June 2019)"); and their provenance or source (e.g., "National Gallery, London" or "Author's own image").

✓ **Be sure to follow appropriate guidance when adding tables, graphs or anything in an appendix**

In science disciplines you are likely to be drawing tables on a relatively frequent basis. You are also likely to have quite clear guidance on the expectations for this, which should be followed. If there is flexibility about how to include graphs or tables, then observe popular stylistic approaches, such as the APA approach (see

Chapter 12). You should not need an appendix unless you need to include additional documents that support your essay and which are referred to as part of the essay, but which do not form part of its main narrative. Examples might include raw data, tables and figures, interview transcripts, maps, images, letters or correspondence, charts, sample surveys and diagrams. However, you must *only* include these if they are referred to in the main body. Also be extremely careful to check if your word count includes appended materials. If so, you may be better off with an extremely brief appendix if any at all. In most cases, and in most disciplines, you will not need one.

✓ **Make sure not to have your name on the script, unless required**

Many assessment instructions are very explicit about not having the candidate's name on the paper. This is to ensure that we can mark as anonymously as possible, without identifying the student behind the work submitted. It helps ensure that the cohort are all marked fairly and consistently, as well as to protect us against unconscious biases or outside influences. It is therefore important, if you are instructed not to put your name and just a candidate number, that you follow this instruction exactly. Similarly, if you are asked to include a word count, then make sure that you add the word count explicitly, exactly as instructed.

✓ **Zoom out to see your paper from a distance**

In terms of structure, formatting and layout, as well as checking the overall presentation of your paper, it is useful to "zoom out" in your word processor (or review it in Print Preview). This enables you to step back and see the shape and layout of all the pages more immediately. It also gives you a real sense of the overall look and feel of your paper. What is more, it helps you spot potential formatting errors or inconsistencies, such as inconsistent margins, alignments, line spacing and font shades. For example, I would leave final fixes or tweaks needed, which I cannot action immediately, in red or in highlight. Then, before I ever finish and send off my work, I would do a final check through on Print

11. Formatting

Preview and will identify the red pen from looking across the document as a whole.

✓ **Follow instructions in terms of file names and uploading**
You have done it! You have now written an *AMAZING* essay. A huge well done! Make sure to follow the exact instructions in terms of how you name your file and upload it into the system. I would say only about 2/3 of students seem to achieve the basic task of naming their essay file correctly! It does not reflect well on the 1/3 who do not follow clear instructions.

So, assuming you do that, and upload it all in time, now it is time give yourself a huge reward. As was discussed in Chapter 4, it is crucial that you really reward yourself for every step and achievement along the way. You deserve it. Well done!

As noted in Chapter 5, because this book contains so much information, I have also produced a helpful checklist booklet to support you. The checklist booklet lists all the key tips and steps that need to be considered at every stage throughout the entire process, acting as an aide-mémoire to everything you have just covered in this book. As noted there, the booklet will not make be any use at all unless you have read this book first! The checklist booklet can be downloaded for free at www.academyworks.co and can be used when you next come to your assignment.

You will also get loads of other super helpful resources for free at that link too, including an essay template, essay timeline calculator, essay process poster and an academic assessment glossary. All you need to do is join my mailing list, but of course you can unsubscribe once you have downloaded the resources. That said, given that I sometimes send out exclusive bonuses, content, offers and resources to my subscribers, you might not want to unsubscribe!

I would also like to take this final moment to ask you to kindly leave a review on Amazon. It takes just a few seconds but makes a huge difference to me. It also helps to support my plans to keep producing further guidance for other students. If you wish to, you may also want to say anything you have found helpful from the book or any of the tips which you will be taking forward. Many thanks—and well done!

12. Further Resources

Online Support

- **Academy Works** (academyworks.co) – The academic skills and studies support platform managed by the author of this book. Includes free resources, templates and materials. Also includes an expert proofreading and editing service where you can get detailed feedback and fixes on your assignment.
- **Grammarly** (grammarly.com) – A very useful and effective grammar-checking service that will spot errors or mistakes in your writing, as well as automatically convert them into more effective prose.
- **Fiverr** (fiverr.com) – A widely respected low-cost freelance platform where you can find a huge range of academic and writing experts who can also proofread your work or provide affordable advice.
- **PeoplePerHour** (peopleperhour.com) – A freelance platform similar to Fiverr.
- **Wyzant** (wyzant.com) – A renowned US-based online tutor platform which advertises the services of many affordable expert tutors in all subject areas.
- **SuperProf** (superprof.co.uk) – A renowned UK-based online tutor platform which advertises the services of many affordable expert tutors in all subject areas.
- **MyTutor** (mytutor.co.uk) – An alternative UK-based online tutor platform.
- **Chegg** (chegg.com) – Chegg is another popular service that provides a bit of a one-stop shop in terms of academic support, with proofreading, tutoring, courses and software all available.

Online Courses and Learning Platforms

- **Academy Works YouTube Channel** (youtube.com/@Academy Works) – The YouTube channel for the publishers of this book series, Academy

Works. More videos and online tutorials will be added frequently. I encourage you to head over and subscribe to the channel to be kept updated on all the latest tips and tricks.

- **Udemy** (udemy.com) – A very popular online short course platform that offers various short unaccredited courses in a range of subjects, usually costing somewhere between $60 to $10. There are frequent promotions that bring the cost of courses down and it offers a 30-day money back guarantee.
- **Coursera** (coursera.com) – A very similar platform to Udemy, with all the same features and benefits, and thousands of other short courses.
- **LinkedIn Learning** (linkedin.com/learning) – A similar platform to Udemy and Coursera. However, LinkedIn Learning tends to be higher quality, higher production cost courses and its pricing can therefore be slightly more.
- **OpenLearn** (open.edu/openlearn) – A free online short course platform covering a range of topics and subjects.
- **FutureLearn** (futurelearn.com) – Another popular online short course platform that offers a range of free and affordable courses in an interesting range of subjects and niche interest topics.

Software and Apps

- **EndNote** (endnote.com) – A very popular referencing management software. Referencing management software has a learning curve and so is perhaps only necessary if you have a lot of academic work in the future. It is also worth checking if your institution has a licence to any software already or if the price can be subsidized in some way.
- **Mendeley** (mendeley.com) – A more detailed and higher specification referencing management software.
- **Citationsy** (citationsy.com) – A popular automated citation app.
- **CiteThisForMe** (citethisforme.com) – Another well-known and widely respected automated citation system.
- **Zotero** (zotero.org) – A free browser extension that many find super helpful for drawing together research materials and resources into one place.

12. Further Resources

- **EverNote** (evernote.com) and **OneNote** (microsoft.com/en-us/micro soft-365/onenote/digital-note-taking-app) – Two popular note-taking apps for task management.
- **Todoist** (todoist.com) or **Any.do** (any.do) – Two popular task management apps. Both can integrate across your apps and platforms, so that you are always able to keep organized at all times.
- **GBoard** (play.google.com/store/apps/details?id=com.google.android.input method.latin&hl=en) – The Google Keyboard app which is free and is a popular dictation (speech-to-text) solution.
- **SimpleMind Lite** (simplemind.eu) – A well-rated mind mapping app and software (not there are many other options on the market too).
- **AppBlock** (appblock.app/students) – A really good and super useful app-blocking solution that can help you to stay focused during "work time". I definitely recommend a solution like this. A similar solution and one which might be even more fun is **Forest** (forestapp.cc). If you manage to resist temptation while working, you can keep adding trees to your own lush forest.

Online Guides and Materials

In all cases you must read the relevant chapter in this book first, as it explains everything in greater detail and with greater accuracy. After reading the relevant chapter, the following unverified resources may offer some additional ideas and suggestions or, in many cases, repeat some aspects of this book using different examples.

Understanding the Assignment

- ❖ How do I Interpret an Essay Question? – University of Cambridge (trans kills.admin.cam.ac.uk/resources/history/essay-writing/how-do-i-interpret-essay-question)

- **Understanding Essay Questions** – University of Canterbury (canterbury.ac.nz/media/documents/academic-skills-centre/Understanding-Essay-Questions.pdf)
- **Video: Academic Writing Webinar** – James Cook University (youtube.com/watch?v=IEicPa6DorY)
- **Understanding Essay Topics: A Checklist** – University of Toronto (advice.writing.utoronto.ca/general/essay-topics)

Common Process Words
- **Academic Assignment Glossary** – Academy Works (academyworks.co)
- **Understanding Essay Questions** – Sheffield Hallam University (blogs.shu.ac.uk/skillscentre/files/2018/10/Handout-Understanding-essay-questions.pdf)
- **Essay Terms Explained** – Bangor University (bangor.ac.uk/studyskills/study-guides/essay-terms.php.en)
- **Understanding Essay Questions** – University of Kent (kent.ac.uk/guides/written-assignments/understanding-essay-questions)

Research
- **Note-taking Techniques** – Open University (help.open.ac.uk/notetaking-techniques)
- **Techniques for Listening and Note-taking** – University of New South Wales (student.unsw.edu.au/notetaking-tips)
- **Introduction to Academic Research** – Sheridan College (Sheridancollege.libguides.com/academic-research)
- **How to do Research: A Step-by-Step Guide** – Elmira College (libguides.elmira.edu/research)
- **Where to Find Scholarly Articles** – Helpful Professor (helpfulprofessor.com/scholarly-articles)

12. Further Resources

- **15 Steps to Good Research** – Georgetown University (library.georgetown.edu/tutorials/research-guides/15-steps)
- **How to do Research for an Excellent Essay** – Oxford Royale (oxford-royale.com/articles/essay-research-skills)

Critical Analysis

- **Critical Analysis: Thinking, Reading and Writing** – University of Reading (libguides.reading.ac.uk/critical-analysis)
- **Critical Thinking** – University of Leeds (library.leeds.ac.uk/info/1401/academic_skills/105/critical_thinking)
- **Critical Analysis** – University of Wollongong (uow.edu.au/student/learning-co-op/assessments/critical-analysis/)
- **A Guide to Critical Writing for Postgraduate Students** – University of Birmingham (intranet.birmingham.ac.uk/as/libraryservices/library/asc/documents/public/pgtcriticalwriting.pdf)

Building Argument

- **Argument** – University of North Carolina (writingcenter.unc.edu/tips-and-tools/argument)
- **Argument and Criticality** – University of Westminster (libguides.westminster.ac.uk/essaywriting/argument)
- **Elements of Persuasive/Argument Papers** – Valencia College (valenciacollege.edu/students/learning-support/winter-park/communications/documents/ElementsofPersuasive.pdf)
- **Building Strong Arguments** – Thoughtful Learning (thoughtfullearning.com/inquireHSbook/pg102)

Planning

- **Essay and Dissertation Writing Skills** – University of Oxford (ox.ac.uk/students/academic/guidance/skills/essay)

- ❖ **Essay Structure** – Harvard College Writing Center (writingcenter.fas.harvard.edu/pages/essay-structure)
- ❖ **Short Guide to Essay Planning & Structure** – University of Birmingham (intranet.birmingham.ac.uk/as/libraryservices/library/asc/documents/public/short-guide-essay-planning.pdf)
- ❖ **7 Steps for Writing an Essay Plan** – Helpful Professor (helpfulprofessor.com/how-to-write-an-essay-plan)

Structure

- ❖ **Essay Structure** – Western Sydney University (westernsydney.edu.au/__data/assets/pdf_file/0016/1082500/Essay_Structure.pdf)
- ❖ **9 Ways to Construct a Compelling Argument** – Oxford Royale (oxford-royale.com/articles/construct-compelling-argument)
- ❖ **Building Argument in an Essay** – James Cook University (jcu.edu.au/__data/assets/pdf_file/0018/1011780/Building-an-Argument-in-an-Essay.pdf)
- ❖ **How to Build an Essay** – Monash University (monash.edu/learnhq/excel-at-writing/how-to-write.../essay/how-to-build-an-essay)
- ❖ **Structure and Flow** – University of Derby (https://libguides.derby.ac.uk/structure-and-flow)

Writing

- ❖ **Grammar, Writing and Notetaking Guide** – Davenport University (davenport.libguides.com/grammar)
- ❖ **Tips & Tools** – UNC Writing Center (writingcenter.unc.edu/tips-and-tools)
- ❖ **Top 20 Errors in Undergraduate Writing** – Stanford University (hume.stanford.edu/resources/student-resources/writing-resources/grammar-resources/top-20-errors-undergraduate-writing)

12. Further Resources

- Top 10 Student Writing Mistakes – Grammarly (grammarly.com/blog/top-10-student-writing-mistakes-finals-edition)
- 10 Typical Essay Writing Mistakes and How to Avoid Them – Skills You Need (skillsyouneed.com/rhubarb/avoid-essay-mistakes)
- 12 Common Essay Writing Mistakes – Capstone Editing (capstoneediting.com.au/blog/12-common-essay-writing-mistakes-youre-still-making)
- 5 Most Common Mistakes in Essay Writing – Writer's Hive (writershivemedia.com/academic-writing/5-most-common-essay-writing-mistakes)

Referencing

- Referencing and Academic Integrity – University of Sussex (sussex.ac.uk/skills-hub/referencing-and-academic-integrity)
- Referencing – Newcastle University (ncl.ac.uk/academic-skillskit/goodacademic-practice/referencing)
- Referencing and Citations – University of Edinburgh (ed.ac.uk/institute-academic-development/study-hub/learning-resources/referencing-and-citations)
- Referencing Explained – University of Leeds (library.leeds.ac.uk/info/1402/referencing/47/referencing_explained)

Formatting

- How Should You Present an Essay? – Bristol University (bristol.ac.uk/media-library/sites/religion/migrated/documents/essayonessay writing.pdf)
- Essay Writing: Formatting – University of Hull (libguides.hull.ac.uk/essays/format)
- Learn the Standard Essay Format: MLA, APA, Chicago Styles – EssayPro (essaypro.com/blog/essay-format)
- How Should I Format My Essay? – Capstone Editing (capstoneediting.com.au/blog/how-should-i-format-my-university-essay)

- **Formatting Your Essay** – University of New England (aso-resources.une.edu.au/wp-content/uploads/2015/08/WE_Formatting-your-essay.pdf)
- **Essay Format: An Easy Writing Guide & Examples** – CollegeEssay.org (collegeessay.org/blog/how-to-write-an-essay/essay-format)

Feedback

- **Short Guide to Using Feedback** – University of Birmingham (intranet.birmingham.ac.uk/as/libraryservices/library/documents/public/15284-ls-short-guide-to-feedback-aw-low-res.pdf)
- **How to Use Assignment Feedback** – Helpful Professor (helpfulprofessor.com/feedback)
- **Feedback: What it is and How to Use it** – University of Bath (bath.ac.uk/guides/feedback-on-your-assignments-what-it-is-and-how-to-use-it)
- **How to Use Your Assignment Feedback** – UWE Bristol (uwe.ac.uk/study/study-support/study-skills/prepare-for-assessments/assessent-feedback#insufficientanalysis)

About the Author

Dr Josh Martin has many years' experience supporting students at leading UK universities. He is a successful lecturer and private tutor, who specializes in helping students to understand complex subjects. He has developed many university courses and has graded and provided feedback on thousands of academic papers. He has also published research in internationally renowned academic journals. *How to Write Amazing Essays* is Dr Martin's first book in Penlyn House's upcoming *Academy Works* series, designed to help students transform their academic performance. More information is available at **academyworks.co**.

Printed in Great Britain
by Amazon